ADVANCE PRAISE

I first heard Andrew speak about the concept of The 4 Keys at a conference in September 2017, and his description of the challenge facing business owners of balancing the four key aspects of business, body, relationships, and mindset in your life massively resonated as I was struggling with an ever-increasing workload, not spending enough quality time with family and friends, making excuses not to exercise, and never switching off. I quickly undertook the Get Fit To Win online training course, joined the Facebook and Get Fit To Win Mastermind (highly recommended for advice, encouragement, and accountability), and set about setting daily, weekly, and monthly targets in each area of my life, which included putting the smartphone in another room in the evenings (not easy!), setting specific time aside at weekends for family time, calling my parents at least once a week, exercising at home if I couldn't get to the gym, introducing myself to a healthier diet and plant-based smoothies, and even going for a walk at lunchtime just to unchain myself from the desk...simple but effective.

I can't recommend The 4 Keys enough or thank Andrew for not only introducing me to the programme but also for providing constant support and encouragement along the way.

—MARK BAKER, DIRECTOR, CLAREMONT CONSULTING
AND CLAREMONT CONSULTING APAC

THE 4 KEYS

THE 4 KEYS

HOW TO WIN IN YOUR BUSINESS, BODY, RELATIONSHIPS, AND MINDSET

ANDREW SILLITOE

LIONCREST
PUBLISHING

THE 4 KEYS

How to Win in Your Business, Body, Relationships, and Mindset

ISBN   978-1-5445-1219-8 *Paperback*
        978-1-5445-1218-1 *Ebook*

To the few, the brave, forward-thinking leaders
who are making real change happen.

#The4Keys

CONTENTS

INTRODUCTION.. 11

PART I: START WITH A VISION

1. THE 4 KEYS 35
2. DEFINE YOUR VISION 57
3. KNOW YOUR WHY 89
4. FIRM YOUR FOUNDATION 105

PART II: TURN YOUR VISION INTO REALITY

5. GET RESULTS FOCUSED 133
6. WIN DAILY... 161
7. MANAGE THE MIST............................. 181

PART III: LIVE YOUR VISION

8. EMBRACE CHANGE............................. 205
9. LEAVE YOUR LEGACY 235

CONCLUSION 243
AFTERWORD...................................... 245
ACKNOWLEDGMENTS 249
ABOUT THE AUTHOR......................... 253

INTRODUCTION

My family had a bakery. Grandad started the business, my father took it over, and every member of my family worked in it. As a child, I loved the bakery and imagined working there my whole life.

I felt safe there, surrounded by family. I remember cleaning down the hot ovens with Brillo Pads, and the feeling of the burn on my knuckles. There is no doubt the bakery air immediately fills you up with the sweet smell of iced buns, Chelsea buns, and cinnamon swirls, and the distinct aroma of dough turning into lightly browned loaves of bread.

There was something magical in that bakery – a place where people worked together for a shared goal and the community rallied around. It was a business an owner could be proud of. Even back then, my entrepreneurial mind was churning, thinking of ways to expand the

business. The bakery had a pizza oven. We could start making pizzas. School kids would line up at lunch time to get slices of fresh, hot pizza.

When I was eleven, a supermarket opened nearby that sold bread. Our business was doing well, despite the competition. Around that same time, a 'friend' persuaded my father to invest in the property business. It was the mid-1980s, and property was booming. I don't know whether my dad was worried about the future of our bakery or intrigued by the prospect of greater wealth, but something lured him away from what three generations of our family had built. My father sold the bakery to pursue construction...and that was the end of my future career as a bakery business owner.

His construction business was profitable, but the family missed working together. Instead, we had a big house and went on vacations in Marbella. My father had a lot of cars, including a beautiful, baby-blue Jaguar E-Type. He worked hard to provide for our family, but the skills that had made the bakery a sustainable financial success didn't translate into the world of construction, and as quickly as my dad made money, he lost it all.

On a Sunday night, 21 March 1993, I was sitting in the living room watching *Rocky V* when my father came in. 'Come and give your dad a hug,' he said.

'No,' I replied.

Three times he asked, and each time I declined. He went off to bed, and that was the last time I saw my father. At 48 years old, Dad died of a heart attack.

Unfortunately, events like this are not uncommon. Stress, anxiety, and the fear of facing work – especially after a weekend of drinking – greatly increase the chances of dying of a heart attack in the early hours of Monday morning. In fact, a ten-year study in Scotland suggested that as many as 20 per cent more people die from heart attacks on Monday than any other day, and a report in the *British Medical Journal* supports the study.[1] I don't want you to feel that way in your business!

My father's death was a devastating moment in my life, but it was also a turning point for me, though I didn't realise it at the time. For years, the running joke in my family has been, 'The only thing Dad left Andrew was his gout,' but in retrospect, my father left me much more.

---

1 'Mondays "Bring Heart Attacks"', *BBC News*, January 20, 2000, accessed September 12, 2018, http://news.bbc.co.uk/2/hi/health/612550.stm.

He inspired me to be an entrepreneur like he was, in a business I could believe in.

Looking back, I believe the way my father lived his life and how he left this earth planted a seed that inspired me to direct my career towards helping people balance their careers, their health, and their relationships. I didn't have a sudden epiphany that Monday morning, but I think that event is what eventually drove me to want to help other business owner like my father, so they didn't suffer the consequences of a life out of balance, like he had.

I grew up playing street hockey in Tunbridge Wells, finished school at an early age, and went to Canada to play. I played inline hockey in 11 championships for Team Great Britain and went on to become the team's head coach. During my four years leading the team, we made history. As head coach, I focused on behaviours over skill, and on creating a culture of high performance. This resulted in my first published book *Managing the Mist: How to Develop Winning Mind-Sets and Create High Performing Teams.*[2]

After several years playing hockey and working in the ski industry, I landed a job at Yellow Pages, which was sort of a crash course in how to be a great employee but also – as

2   Andrew Sillitoe, *Managing the Mist: How to Develop Winning Mind-Sets and Create High Performing Teams* (St Albans: Panoma, 2013).

a salesperson dependent on selling for my income – how to be responsible for my own time and success.

I had my first daughter, Izzie, at 22 years old, and I became a single parent when she was six. At the time, I was consulting with over 20 businesses per week over a four-year period, and I couldn't help but empathise with the business owners. They were working overtime, having challenges not only managing their businesses but also the other facets of their lives – just like my dad and his failing health.

I left Yellow Pages in 2007 to train as an executive coach and pursue a career as a performance coach. I attended evening classes at university, and in 2012, I got a master's degree in organisational psychology. That same year, as a business psychologist, I started a consultancy, The Strategic Team Coach, and began working with executive teams. The lessons I had learnt as a hockey player and coach, coupled with my education and my experience, transferred well to my consultancy business. Still, something was missing.

The last ten years have been a powerful journey for me – building an online training company, speaking all over the world, and advising leaders in FTSE 100 companies. I talked about my years in hockey and about creating a high-performance, winning culture, which was what business executives wanted to hear. But for many of those years, I wasn't dealing with the most important element in these people's lives – the human element.

A business coach cannot simply give people rules to follow and steps to take that will turn them into high-performing teams. For that to happen, real conversations need to take place. It's more than checking a box or satisfying a requirement for the human resources department. Business people are human beings first, with real, human problems. Failing to acknowledge, discuss, and address their issues – not just as entrepreneurs, leaders, or employees, but as people – ignored the most important aspect of how high-performance teams are created.

EARLY MISSTEPS

I didn't get there right away. Instead, I followed in Dad's footsteps at first, working too much and neglecting everything else. My dad had often half-jokingly referred to alcohol as his 'medicine', and whilst I didn't consider it to be mine, I had adopted hockey as my antidote to stress, but not in a good way. I was obsessed with it, whether I was playing or coaching. Also, like my father, I didn't realise the damage that single-minded focus was causing to my health and to my relationships. I didn't have a heart attack, but I suffered greatly in other parts of my life.

There's a fine line between passion and obsession. The over-the-top dedication that comes with an obsession throws your life off balance, and the sacrifices you make to pursue that obsession come at a detriment to your business, health, and relationships. Chasing a passion in a more relaxed, enjoyable, and even playful way allows for more balance in other parts of your life, so you can succeed in each facet. This is what I have learnt more recently, but back then, my hockey obsession was chipping away at my life.

My big wake-up call happened in 2017. While my wife was visiting her family in Prague, she called to say she was leaving me.

I was totally blindsided but shouldn't have been. Conversations were taking place, but I was ignoring them. More than once my wife had said, 'I didn't sign up for this,' referring to my workaholic lifestyle, the difficult relationship with Izzie's mother, and my only outlet/obsession – hockey. Each time, I dismissed the comment, telling myself I had launched my consultancy business and was working hard to provide for our family: 'It's just hockey.' I told myself she should have known what she was getting into when she married me.

These are the sorts of things you tell yourself when you don't want to face the truth. Facing the truth means you have to deal with the problem, and I was too busy for that and too busy to imagine the consequences of my choices. I should have listened to my wife and taken her comments seriously. I should have given her a hug and made changes to get my life in balance.

Instead, I tried to defend myself. 'We go out,' I said. 'We spend time together.'

'Yes,' she replied. 'We go out, but you're never really there. I'm there in front of you, but you're thinking about work or hockey.'

She left me, and this was not a simple breakup, if there is such a thing. Izzie is my wife's stepdaughter, and the two of them have a very close relationship. Not only had it become a strain on them, but my relationship with Izzie was also suffering. My wife and I also had two young children together. In my mind, my career and the money it provided was all they needed from me – all that was required of me to be a good husband and father. Writing these words now, I see how utterly foolish that sounds. I wasn't being present with my wife or with my children. I was not being the man they needed me to be for them or the man I needed to be for myself. These are issues I had to deal with. They were the most important issues of my life, and I'm still dealing with them.

Looking back at my life, I can see the connections between events that happened long ago and how I deal with issues as an adult. There's this dream that I have in which my father returns. This time, I don't tell him to go away. I wrap my arms around him and don't let go, and I cry so much. I wake up in tears, emotionally wrecked. Years later, as an adult, other people have needed me: my wife, my family. I haven't always been there for them, not in the way they needed me to be. It was too easy to tell them to buck up, be strong, thinking, *Can't they see how hard I'm working? How I'm doing all this for them?* When what they really needed was a damn hug.

If it seems like I'm getting off track a bit here, hang in there with me. This part matters. We all have experiences that shape our lives and our behaviours, and not always for the better. Some behaviours serve us, and others can sabotage our lives. We're not locked into these behaviours and patterns that don't serve us. We can change them. First, we must identify them, and then we can do something about them.

AN EPIPHANY

One day, shortly after my wife had moved out, I was on my way to a conference in Ibiza. I was thinking about my message and how many of the audience had heard my talk about leadership, building teams, and the parallels in sport.

The business leaders I met with wanted to know about running a business, and that's what I always talked about. I also spoke to them briefly about the importance of a healthy mindset and high performance because I knew these things affected business results and success. Still, *something was missing.*

That's when it hit me: I had been following my own advice - taking care of my mindset and building a successful business - yet I had been neglecting my health and the most important relationships in my life, and it was affecting everything else. How could I maintain a peaceful state of mind and run my business when I was feeling so fatigued all the time and all I could think about were my wife and kids? How could I stand up in front of a roomful of people and ignore the elephant in the room, the elephant in my head?

I got up on stage at that conference and took a huge risk - a leap of faith. Instead of launching into my prepared speech, I told these people what was on my mind.

'Listen,' I said, 'you're all business owners. You've come to this conference because you want to grow a business. You want to make it sustainable. I can almost guarantee that you've all told your husbands and wives that you've got a three-year plan and it's all going to come out great and you'll have that financial freedom and security in three years' time.

'Here's what's going to happen: at the end of that three years, your partner will leave you – possibly for a person who's paid them more attention than you have, but more likely because he or she is simply tired of coming *last* – behind your business, your team, your colleagues, and your clients – on your list of 'priorities'. Your health will have deteriorated because you focused all your energy on your business. Your relationship with your kids will be toxic. I'm betting none of that's in your three-year plan, but that's how it will play out.

'Here's what we're going to do. I am looking for a group of people to join me on a pilot programme. I need five people, and we're going to work out every day. We're going to meditate. We're going to think about our families and what we can do to maintain and enrich those relationships, and we're going to think about our businesses and how we manage that. Who would like to join me in this small group and work with me over 90 days? Can I have five volunteers?'

Ten hands went up. By the end of the conference, 15 people had committed to join me on this plan.

I came away from the conference thinking, *There's something to this. This is connecting with these people.* I wasn't preaching this stuff; I was experiencing it with them and learning from other members in the group. Within six weeks, we had over 200 members in my Facebook group, called Get Fit To Win.

We developed a 90-day game plan, a *reset*, with 30- and 60-day benchmarks to create some urgency and keep us focused. After completing the 90-day plan, we took a break, and started a second one. The results give me goosebumps even today as I sit here telling you this. The participants have lost weight, are happier, and their businesses are doing well. More importantly, their relationships are thriving. These people who joined me in the 90-Day Reset plan introduced me to their spouses and took selfies with me. They wanted their families to know who I was.

This was how the Get Fit To Win brand was launched, and *The 4 Keys* programme was born.

WHY I BELIEVE IN THE PROGRAMME AND IN YOU

I'm a firm believer that living with purpose, the journey you experience, and the lives you impact is a true measure of your wealth. Having competed and coached sports at an elite level, I realised early on that when we commit to a vision and pursue it with 100 per cent passion, anything is possible.

If my father taught me one thing, living a life with purpose is far more important to me than working on something I don't fully understand or love just to survive, make money, and then die.

By following simple steps daily and making lifestyle changes, my clients have transformed their marriages and other personal relationships. They are healthier, stronger, and mentally tougher, and their businesses are thriving. Already, hundreds of participants in *The 4 Keys* programme have become the best version of themselves and, more importantly, are inspiring others to be the best version of themselves.

I want this for you, and I know it's possible. From my first taste of entrepreneurship at the bakery to my professional career to launching my own consultancy, I've seen what can go right – and wrong – with running a business. I have a genuine empathy for business owners and executives, and a burning desire to see them succeed. I suppose this started early, watching my father's professional rise and fall, and it grew as I worked with clients at Yellow Pages – four or five entrepreneurs a day – helping them grow their businesses. As a business consultant, I've coached more than 2,000 people and have been moved

THE GREATEST REWARD: A CLIENT'S LIFE-CHANGING RESULTS

There's nothing more rewarding than hearing from people who have participated in *The 4 Keys* programme and want to share their experiences. Through their own efforts, and by being their own catalysts for change, they have achieved life-altering results. One of my clients, Brian Johnson, shared this story of how the 90-day programme affected his personal and professional life.

"As a former professional sportsman (Rugby Union, as my back reminds me daily) and now business owner/operator, I am well-versed in goal setting, getting the balance right between strategy and daily tactics, and driving performance. What I hadn't realised was that all the different parts of your life can be brought together into one salient plan, with a joined-up approach and in a focused amount of time. Going through *The 4 Keys* programme with Andrew allowed me to assess where I was at that time and understand how adrift I was from my overall goals. I had become too focused on the detail of daily business performance, forgetting the longer-term approach. I had forgotten to take care of my mindset, health, and nutrition, and I had let my efforts around relationships slip. Working through *The 4 Keys* gave me a genuine sense of excitement as I got everything back on track. I'm almost 90 days through the programme and most telling is that my relationship with my wife is amazing. She can see that I am happier, healthier, and less stressed. I am more present with her (and everyone else I deal with) and work is benefiting from my new energy levels and focus. I didn't know that I needed a bit of an overhaul, but meeting Andrew and working with him over the last three months has been genuinely life changing."

—BRIAN JOHNSON

by their stories. You don't work with that many businesses and come away untouched by the people. I witnessed many successes, but I saw plenty of failures: declining health, stress, deteriorating personal relationships. I began to care deeply for struggling business owners and wanted to help them, but I knew it would take more than the traditional business advice I was offering.

My commercial experience, combined with research and what I learnt at university, provided a solid foundation for my consultancy. However, my education did not, and could never, replace my first-hand experiences with people who want to run a successful business, feel stuck, and don't know why. Until you've worked with people who are doing everything right in business yet sacrificing everything else in their lives, you cannot understand the consequences of a life half-lived, the lost opportunities for a balanced life, and the impact it has on their business, body, relationships, and mindset.

Behind every strong business are strong relationships. Marriages, families, partnerships, and relationships with colleagues and friends all affect how you show up in your career.

Your physical health, state of mind, and the people in your life – and how you interact with them – affect your business. Issues with my relationships had crept into my head when I was away at hockey tournaments, interrupted my thoughts when I was travelling for speaking engagements, and distracted me on the way to that particular conference. You might think you can turn relationship problems off, but you can't, and they affect the other parts of your life. Even if you could compartmentalise these things somehow, why would you want to? Having a healthy body and mind is important. Having healthy relationships is important. As much as we focus on business, these other key factors are not only critical to our lives, but they are also critical to our business success.

I started my business thinking entrepreneurs needed advice on coaching, leadership, business psychology, and all those things I had learnt at university and in my professional career. They do. But what they really needed – and weren't getting – were lessons on health, relationships, and mindset, and how these factors manifested themselves in their professional performance.

THE 4 KEYS

I created the Get Fit To Win brand and *The 4 Keys* programme to enable business owners and leaders to thrive. The online programme – and this book – aren't about inspiring you to grow your business so you can have all the materialistic things you want in life or about spending excessive time at the gym, sticking to a restrictive diet, or sitting cross-legged on the floor for hours, contemplating life. They're about holding the mirror up to yourself and asking, 'What is it I'm doing, or not doing, as a human being? How can I do better? What can I do today to do better, to be better?' As a result, you may make different choices about how you fuel your body, stay strong, balance your relationships, and improve mental toughness.

As businesspeople, this isn't natural. It's not natural for me. The entrepreneurial mindset is, 'I can make a go of this – just watch me!' and the entrepreneur's natural behaviour is to project that same attitude onto everyone around them. However, what you view as acceptable expectations aren't always fair to others or even to yourself. Asking your spouse and your children to forgo a normal family life in support of your professional aspirations isn't fair to them. Asking your friends and colleagues to want the same thing you want and to commit to it as wholeheartedly as you commit to it isn't fair. Yet these behaviours are all too common for business owners and leaders. Every person has their own values and their own visions of what they want their life to be, and being a better human requires us to respect those values and visions – those passions, purposes, and desired outcomes of the people with whom we surround ourselves.

Managing the health of our bodies and our mindsets doesn't come naturally to business leaders either. We believe we can thrive on any diet and any exercise programme (or none), yet these behaviours affect us in ways we may not be aware. It's not possible to run your business at 100 per cent if your health is struggling.

You can change, though. Wherever you are in life, you can change your beliefs and your behaviours, and you can win at business, body, relationships, and mindset and create a balanced fitness across each facet of your life.

This is an ongoing process built on a firm foundation. You have to be vulnerable, and you have to be brave. You must be willing to keep going and be open to the possibility of enormous success. Even for me, the author of this book, it's an ongoing process, but with each day, there are more failures from which to learn and more successes to celebrate.

This isn't a three-year plan. You don't have that kind of time, and frankly, neither does your business, body, relationships, or your mindset. This is a 90-day plan that you can start right away. You can read this book and then start, or you can finish this chapter and start today. I do hope you will read through to the end. I have many stories to share that will inspire you and show you why this works, how this works, and what's possible in just three months' time.

To help guide you, this book has three parts: 'Start with a Vision', 'Turn Your Vision into Reality', and 'Live Your Vision'. We'll begin in Part 1 by getting clear about your vision and your purpose across *The 4 Keys*: business, body, relationships, and mindset. You will have to ask yourself, 'What am I doing, and why am I doing it? What is my purpose in this life? In this business?' Then we'll look ahead to the future, and you will ask yourself, 'Where am I going? Where do I want to be in 12 months, three years, five years, or even 20 years? What do I want to see, hear, and feel across my business, body, relationships, and mindset?' Consider them all, because they are inter-related, and each one affects the others. You're going to think big, be a little deluded, and maybe even scare your-self with your vision.

From there, we're going to turn your vision into reality by getting focused and results-driven. In Part 2, we'll unpack your vision into a 90-Day Reset. You'll identify 30- and 60-day benchmarks across *The 4 Keys*. Then we'll talk about how you get there day by day. By focus-ing on the daily wins, the benchmarks and the outcomes will happen.

In Part 3, we'll look at how to live your vision by exploring how you could be getting in your own way and how to identify any changes you want make. I'll be asking you to think deeply about how your life is playing out based on past experiences and ingrained patterns, and while this is not a book about therapy, you may want to consider the effects of these experiences and patterns and what you need to do to move forward.

This isn't magic, and there is work involved, but you can

master each of *The 4 Keys* – business, body, relationships, and mindset. You can rebuild yourself and your business and open the door to success.

Your vision and purpose matter. Never forget that. But you must learn the framework, skills, and tools to create your own legacy.

PART I

START WITH A VISION

CHAPTER 1

THE 4 KEYS

The challenge of work-life balance is without question one of the most significant struggles faced by modern man.

—STEPHEN COVEY

When I began my executive coaching career, my work focused on business and leadership. I wasn't a life coach, although the personal side of my clients' lives would often come up in the coaching conversation. I tended to keep the conversations professional. As I dived into coaching, I became fascinated with the role of leadership, not just those I was coaching but also my own role leading consulting teams and elite sports teams. I began to examine other leaders in business, politics, and sports, from Nelson Mandela to Sir Alex Ferguson, looking for common traits and other similarities. The connection between leadership, mindset, and physical health was apparent in business success, yet at the time, I hadn't identified the final, vital element for true success – relationships.

While I was prepping for the speaking engagement in Ibiza, *The 4 Keys* and their connections to each other became clear to me. I didn't script my speech that day; I spoke from my heart. I didn't worry about what my audience might think, and I was willing to take a risk by changing up my speech. My words resonated with them, and the message started to spread. People started to use the language immediately. They started referring to *The 4 Keys* and how important they are to balance. Members in the audience tweeted about my talk using the hashtag #The4Keys. I realised straight away this could change lives.

Ultimately, my newfound willingness to embrace the personal as well as the professional side of executives' lives made me a better coach, and I could finally offer my clients all the tools they needed to help them achieve success – *The 4 Keys*: business, body, relationships, and mindset.

BUSINESS

During my career, I have created a number of different businesses. It is fair to say I made a lot of mistakes along the way. My management career started in retail. I left school at 16 with a handful of GCSEs. What I lacked in academic ability, I made up in ambition and drive. (I didn't have a choice.) I had a number of jobs, from selling suits on the East London markets, managing a sports shop, and running my own sports development company to selling skis. I had even spent some time laying tarmac on the streets of my local town before joining Yellow Pages.

My leadership career didn't start well. I cringe at some the behaviours I displayed. I challenge anyone who says creating a business and managing results through others is easy. I have had moments of greatness, been okay, and been absolutely clueless. Building a business is hard. The sooner you accept this, the better leader you will become. The mistake I made was pretending it was easy and that I had it nailed. Whether you're a one-man band, a team of ten, or leading an organisation of 80,000 employees, leading a profitable and sustainable business is one of the most rewarding and satisfying things you can undertake. Leadership is a way of life and a constant work in progress.

The business key involves thinking about the business *you want to create*. Take a moment to consider these questions. What does the business look like? How big is it, and how big is your team? What's your turnover? What market do you work in, and what do you offer? What's your role in this business, and where do you see yourself and your business in three years?

For many business owners, the biggest challenge is letting go. Stepping back and letting someone else take responsibility for an element of their company – whether that's as CEO, head of sales, performing the service you're offering, or a mixture of all those things – in the form of a new business partner. If you plan to scale your business, you must let go of something to experience meaningful growth.

Take a moment to ask yourself, does the idea of being CEO excite you? Or would you rather bring in another CEO and focus on sales? You don't have to answer these questions yet; we'll get into that later. For now, just think about them. Once you know where you want to be, you'll figure out what you need to do to get there. Then you can take action to make your dreams a reality.

Also consider your lifestyle goals and financial rewards. Does your business allow you to travel? Pursue your hobbies? Enjoy your ideal lifestyle? In this business you want to create, how much money are you taking out of the business? If there isn't enough profit in a business just yet, an owner may have to take less salary than some of their employees until the business grows. Establish your desired remuneration, then figure out what you need to do to get there. The 90-Day Reset plan will help guide you through the steps to achieve your desired outcome.

BODY

The body key is not about diet and body building. It is about lifestyle and about how you want to feel, both physically and mentally.

I come from a sporty family, and I was always interested in sport, psychology, and performance, probably because my father had been a good football player and cricket player. Also, my sister Joanne played field hockey for the county and represented England. This inspired me to test myself at an early age playing street hockey. (I broke my arm three times learning to skate.) My mother bought me my first hockey stick when I was nine. In a way, it represented freedom for me, because having my own stick meant I could play anywhere, anytime. I didn't have to borrow a stick from someone else. Getting that hockey stick and experiencing that sense of freedom was a pivotal moment in my life. By age 11, I was playing street hockey every day in the local car parks and school playgrounds, skating to school, and travelling to London to watch games. My mother was always interested in skating and loved hockey. She still does, and she watches more hockey than I do! Her support has been a huge influence on my playing career and developing a positive attitude towards sport.

I didn't engage in sports in high school at first. I was a chubby kid, and you could say I had a predisposition to being overweight. 'It's just puppy fat, Andrew; you'll grow out of it' was often the response to my frustration regarding my weight, although I think it had more to do with growing up in a bakery! Playing hockey changed how I felt about sports and gave me confidence. Finally, even though I wasn't as muscular as some of the other boys in school, I felt like I had an edge. I dreamt of playing street hockey to the highest level possible. I was fortunate that my dad's best friend 'Jock' (the only Scotsman in Tunbridge Wells!) had a gym in his garage, and as a 15-year-old, I trained seriously with him and his two sons, Darren and John. When my father passed, Jock became like a godfather to me.

Jock wasn't vain, but he'd often say that you look better in your clothes when you work out, and the truth of that stuck with me. He taught me about weight training, mental toughness, and specific sports training. The effort resulted in me representing the London All-Stars, the top 12 players in the country, and experiencing an all-expenses paid trip to Florida at 17 years old.

Unfortunately, in those days, training was designed to hurt. 'No pain, no gain' was the mantra, combined with a high-carb diet of pasta, bread, and sugary sports drinks that led to feeling tired, injured, and inflamed. This went on for 15 years and although I was strong and fit, I was aching all over and felt tired all the time. It turns out I was suffering with an autoimmune disease called gout, a form of inflammatory arthritis characterised by recurrent attacks in the joints. It is extremely painful, although at the time, I assumed I'd injured myself playing or overdone it in the gym.

Over time, the gouty arthritis became chronic, with regular attacks sometimes lasting four to six weeks. This caused my early retirement from playing hockey at a high level. The pain forced me to cancel work engagements and leadership programmes. As a business owner, you cannot afford time off work. The problem with an autoimmune disease is that it doesn't just affect the joints, it also affects the mind. I would feel very low and depressed, and this would affect my personal relationships. Also, having lost my father to a sudden heart attack, I was even more conscious of the health implications, especially knowing that inflammatory diseases can lead to Type 2 diabetes and heart disease.

In 2006 I was also diagnosed with hip arthritis and was told that I would have to have my hip replaced within five to ten years. Clearly, I was ruining my immune system and my joints, stressing my body with too much exercise and eating an inflammatory diet. But the doctors didn't have any answers; in fact, they sniggered about my gout as 'the rich man's disease'. Remember, my family had joked that gout was the only thing my dad left me, and he suffered with it terribly. That's when I started exploring nutrition as a way to enhance my well-being and improve my immune system. I wanted to understand the causation rather than take the prescription drugs offered to me by my doctor.

While I was unable play anymore, I could certainly coach, and I did. I spent four years coaching Team GB at the World Championships, where we gained promotion into Pool A for the first time, competing against the top eight countries in the world. The success of Team GB inspired me to write *Managing the Mist*.

By this point, I had learnt about nutrition, I'd removed grains and sugar from my diet, and learnt how to manage my arthritis. The inflammatory attacks started to become less often, and I started working out again. I got back into playing hockey regularly, making a return in 2014 and representing both the men's team in the Pool A World Championships and GB Vets (38 and over) World Championships.

Now, at 42, I feel stronger, fitter and leaner than I was at 22. I am so grateful for the knowledge I have that has allowed me to be my best at work mentally and physically and still play hockey. It's hard to imagine the pain I was in back then and how debilitating it was.

I draw on my extensive research into nutrition and training, my certification as a health coach, and my own experiences to design an approach aimed at busy business owners and leaders like you who want to get strong, lean, and healthy, and to live an energised, happy, and enjoyable life.

Out of writing this book, *The 4 Keys*, came the Get Primal programme and the inaugural Get Fit To Win Retreat, a three-day retreat bringing together entrepreneurs and business leaders in the Get Fit To Win community for a weekend of amazing food, great company, business ideas, breakout sessions, and a little training and relaxation.

My life has been one built around sports, health, and fitness, and I have managed to create a lifestyle rather than stick to a boring, restrictive diet. I've made it my personal goal to help one million business leaders take full responsibility in their business, body, relationships, and mindset.

I encourage you to discover how easy wellness can be for a business leader by managing three basic needs: nutrition, exercise, and rest. I provide a complete eating, exercise, and lifestyle philosophy, along with various products, services, and incredible support from the Get Fit To Win community.

Nutrition is very personal, so this is not a one-size-fits-all solution; however, I am a strong advocate of keeping it simple, eating healthy fats, moderate protein, and carbohydrates aligned to your level of activity. I'll also provide you with simple and effective training programmes that will get you looking and feeling great. I've learnt two important things about exercise: (1) you cannot out-train a bad diet, and (2) you don't need to train excessively or even consistently (despite popular belief) to get fit, lean, and strong.

You can change your life, increase the energy you need to create a thriving business, be the leader you aspire to be, and be a role model to others. You'll get strong and lean, and it will seem effortless and enjoyable by following some simple steps.

I love hearing stories about how my life served as an incentive for others to change their own lives. For example, my client Robert Bruce had gained weight and wasn't happy about it, but he'd lost the motivation to train. He watched my TEDx Talk, and it touched him. Robert realised that he was on an unhealthy trajectory. He has children, too, so the question 'What kind of legacy do you want to leave?' really resonated with Robert. More than the financial stability of instituting all four keys for business success, he saw the importance of his legacy and the lessons and values he was teaching his kids. My talk was a catalyst for change for Robert, and after 90 days, here's what he had to say: 'My business partner and I embraced *The 4 Keys*. We're in the shape of our lives as a business, as individuals. For a 45-year-old man who was extremely unfit 12 weeks ago, it proves what can be achieved when you go all in.'

While there will always be an element of vanity (hey, we all want to look good, right?), body is more about how you feel.

Reflect on these questions. We'll discuss them in greater detail later on, but for now, just give them some thought. How do you fuel your body, and how does it feel? How does your competence and ability fluctuate throughout the day? What is your body goal?

Your goal should be about more than how you look, such as 'I want a six pack.' We're not doing a 90 Days to Ripped Abs or a Whole-Body Transformation here. Instead, look at losing some weight and toning up as a by-product of the body key, which combines physical activity and conscious nutrition. The programme helps you make better, more informed nutritional choices and encourages you to get your heart rate up for short periods every day.

I don't expect you to be doing 200 push-ups twice a day right out of the gate, because that's a pretty overwhelming prospect for most people. But getting your heart rate up every day, even if it's only for five minutes at a time, is hugely beneficial, and it's within reach for everyone. If you've got the time and the motivation to do an hour or more in the gym every day, then do it, but for many people, that just isn't possible. Everyone can, however, find five or ten minutes at least once a day to get some high-intensity activity in. See how many sets of squats and sit-ups of ten reps each you can squeeze into five minutes, for example.

Our bodies haven't changed much over the millennia, and we're designed to be nomads who walk 12 miles a day. In this modern era, some people don't even walk one mile a day. We've become increasingly sedentary since the Industrial Revolution, so while our life styles have improved, they've also become increasingly unhealthy.

Your exercise should be in balance with the rest of your life, so always leave some energy for other activities. Move slowly, and don't overdo it with heavy lifting to failure, which can be counterproductive. Overtraining can put your body under a lot of stress and accelerate the ageing process. Instead of going all out every time, make working out part of your lifestyle and always leave something 'in the tank' so you can enjoy all your life. Exercise shouldn't leave you exhausted. It should energise you.

Getting the body key right and following through with it

every day doesn't just have an impact on your physical fitness. It's also good for your energy and your mindset. They're all linked. When we exercise, our bodies release chemicals, including endorphins that increase serotonin, which is linked to happiness. Activity is a vital part of our day. You feel healthier, happier, and more energised when you're active, and you're more productive, so you end up with more time for your relationships.

Body is also about nutrition. I won't give you a strict diet to follow, because we're all different. But I will provide you with some guiding principles and help you educate yourself and find the diet that works for you, whether it's paleo, keto, Mediterranean, vegetarian, or something else altogether. Your best diet is whatever works for you: what gives you energy and improved cognitive function. Moreover, if you have an inflammatory problem, Crohn's disease, or IBS, the right diet plan can quite simply change your life.

RELATIONSHIPS

Winning at life demands attention to your business, body, relationships, and mindset, and you can't neglect any of them. Sometimes, that's a challenge. Many of us who appear to be successful in our work, happy, and in good health, unconsciously neglect our relationships. Instead of being accountable for our role in this behaviour, we tend to blame the relationship itself or the other people in the relationship.

What I have learnt in recent years is that to have an amazing relationship with someone else, we have to first have a great relationship with ourselves. If we don't have a great relationship with ourselves, it is very likely that we will continue repeating patterns that could be dysfunctional.

Consider these questions. We'll talk about them more in the coming chapters, but for now, give them some thought. How much quality time do you spend with your partner, and how is that relationship? Do you know what motivates them? How are your own personal motivations helping or hindering your relationship with your partner? How do you want your partner to experience you? How do you want the relationship to feel? How do you want to feel in that relationship? Maybe you are already passionate about your work and you understand how to fuel your body and work out every day. Do you understand your relationships, or put the same effort into them? How much effort *do* you put in? After you reflect on these questions, think about the actions you can take to bring you both closer.

The relationship key goes beyond partners to include other family members, colleagues, and friends. The health of your relationships impacts your physical health, your mindset, and your business, and is a crucial factor in business success.

When I was single, one of my main relationship issues was settling down too soon. I'd start a relationship that wasn't really right for me, but I'd stick with it, thinking it would eventually get better. A lot of this had to do with trying to find the right stepmother for Izzie rather than waiting to find the right person for me.

Settling was easier than doing something about a relationship that didn't serve me, and it became a pattern of behaviour. Many of us engage in repeated behaviours that don't serve us. Instead, we should take a step back, identify these behaviours, and examine them more closely. Then we can decide which ones serve us and which don't, and make decisions about them that may be hard in the short term but will deliver more positive long-term results.

Once I was married, my greatest relationship challenge was prioritising the people who were most important in my life: my family. If you're like many busy executives, you know your relationships are important, but they're not urgent, so you don't prioritise them. Date night gets bumped, a trip with the kids gets cancelled, or you don't book that holiday because a work commitment came in. None of these events are urgent, so you often cancel them without concern. Then, one day, your partner says, 'I didn't sign up for this. I'm taking the kids, and we're leaving you.' Suddenly, maintaining those relationships is very urgent. You could have planned ahead and been proactive, but now you have to react.

A strong relationship key is crafted by putting greater emphasis on those relationships and being proactive about developing them. Don't cancel movie night with your kids or date night with your spouse for anything less than a catastrophe. Set aside plenty of family time where you put away phones and tablets and just be present in that relationship. Your kids don't care about the expensive watch or the brand-new Range Rover. They just want you, and they won't be young forever. Soon they'll be teenagers. How do you want them to remember their childhood? What kind of role model do you want to be for them?

And if, as was my experience, a long-term relationship moves past urgent and you find you're on the verge of getting divorced, you can still adopt these techniques to make sure you and your partner are still close and have a good, heathy relationship at the centre and with the children.

MINDSET

In 2007 a consultancy that specialises in improving business performance asked me to deliver a keynote speech on the parallels between sports and business performance at one of their team-building days. The COO of the consultancy at the time was an old school friend of mine, and despite the fact we had not spoken in 20 years, he had been following my sports career. I grew up playing a relatively unknown sport, especially by English standards, where most young children aspire to play football for England. I've had an unusual albeit successful sports career competing and coaching roller hockey all over Europe and throughout the United States and Canada at both club and international level.

However, despite my experiences, when I sat down to write the speech, it occurred to me that I wasn't entirely sure what the parallels were. I knew what I had done to achieve my goals and the sacrifices I had made. Coping with the fear of failure at times had become overwhelming, but I wasn't clear on how to express that in an inspirational and practical way. Growing up in a sporting environment, I understood from an early age that physical fitness and a healthy mindset go hand-in-hand. I was fortunate that Jock had introduced me to several books on mindset at a young age. These methods provided me with the tools and techniques I needed later in my career in both sports and entrepreneurialism.

I sat down in a cafe with some strong coffee and started to write the speech. I had never been a person who excelled at writing essays or perceived myself as academic in any way; however, on this occasion, I was like Forest Gump, but instead of running, I was writing, and I kept writing and writing. More writing and research eventually resulted in my first published book *Managing the Mist* in 2013.

After 15 years of working with business leaders and owners, I have come to the conclusion that there are three key principles for developing the right mindset for success. Firstly, those who possess what I call 'the winning mindset' have a high level of self-awareness; they know their strengths and weaknesses, motivations, and what stresses them internally and externally. Secondly, they have the ability to use their self-awareness to manage their thoughts, feelings, and emotions under pressure. Thirdly, they are goal-orientated and have a plan for achieving their goals.

I have learnt that having the right mindset is essentially an attitude of mind. With the right mindset, you will live, work, and compete at your full potential. Virtually everything you do in your life is ruled by choices that you make. You can choose to focus on the negative or the positive, you can get stressed about things beyond your control, or you can focus on the things that you can influence.

An obstacle can be a barrier to performance or it can be an opportunity to learn and improve. These choices will have a direct impact on your performance and well-being.

Mindset is a combination of aggressive action, focus, and inner peace. Think of the Special Air Service (SAS) or the Navy Seals. They have mastered the art of aggressive action coupled with intense focus and utterly calm composure. Consider basketball players who display aggressive action with their explosive movements yet are able to compose themselves to make a game-winning shot. Mindset is about taking action and composing ourselves under pressure and harnessing our thoughts and emotions in chaotic or intense situations.

When you're in sports, you practise every day but only play a win-lose game once or twice a week. In business, you're in a win-lose situation every day, and there is no practice. Every day is a case of 'Did I win or lose?' Establishing the right mindset quickly is crucial. Yes, you need to focus on the day-to-day activities, but you also need to prepare yourself by being proactively mindful, as an athlete would for a championship game.

Identifying activities and interactions that make you stressed, anxious, or angry is a great place to start, so you can eliminate them from your life or learn how to manage them. Breathing and meditative exercises designed to relax the nervous system help give you that control and inner peace. When my clients adopted these techniques, they became calmer and less egotistical, which in turn benefited their physical health and relationships.

Preparing yourself mentally helps you find peace and calm in all facets of your life and empowers you to get through intense, stressful situations without resorting to fight-or-flight mode. Imagine driving a car at high speed and you see you're hitting a tight bend too fast, so you slam on the brakes, and your car spins as you lose control. This is reactivity, which leads to less-intelligent choices. Now look at the same scenario from a proactive stance. You're driving a car at high speed, and you see a bend ahead. You slow down on the approach, then, as you hit the bend, you accelerate through it, coming back onto the straight road on the other side, in complete control. If you can see something coming, you can plan for it and turn it into a success.

WINNING AT LIFE

We're all normal people navigating the game of life as best we can, and *The 4 Keys* will show you how to achieve success in all aspects of your life. This book isn't about helping you make material gains; it's about helping you figure out what's really important to you and becoming more mindful so you can work towards winning at life – your life. Does boasting about your huge house and pool in the garden make you happy, or does the matching, enormous mortgage keep you up at night? Is the ego massage, and influence over other people's perceptions of you, worth that hefty monthly lease on the latest, most expensive home entertainment system? Might you be happier with a smaller mortgage and car payment, along with less stress and more time to enjoy your life and spend time with your kids?

My goal is to help you find a balance of improvement and enjoyment. Thirty days into my 90-Day Reset plan, you may find yourself looking forward to your next 90-day plan, like some of my clients did. During my own first 90 days, I continued running my business, launched another business, built a website, and began writing this book. I've done everything I set out to do and more. The plan takes you out of your comfort zone for 90 days at a time, after which you go back to your comfort zone as a better version of yourself and with a comfort zone much bigger than it was before you started the plan. After your 90-Day Reset, you sustain your new comfort zone, then, when you're ready, you stretch yourself with another 90 days. If you do just one 90-day plan a year, you'll reap massive benefits, but you may want to do it twice a year, or more.

The plan isn't designed to make you miserable. It's tailored to your needs and your abilities, and it's flexible. If you're having a bad week, and you can't face getting up at 5 a.m. tomorrow, then don't. Trust your intuition and get up a little later, skip the meditation or the workout, and spend a bit more time with the kids, go for a slow walk, or do something else that you love. You won't have to give up everything you enjoy either. If you really like eating a Big Mac once a week, I won't ask you to stop eating hamburgers, but I will encourage you to add something a little healthier to your routine, such as a five-minute workout every day and a date night once a week. Does that sound horrible?

You don't even have to focus on every key in every 90-day plan that you do. You could decide you're happy with where your business is right now, but you know you need to work on your relationships or your body, so you just focus on those. You create your own roadmap to achieve real results and long-term rewards.

The 4 Keys is about enjoying life as much as making improvements. It's about listening to your body and your mind and making better choices for a better life. Following this plan gradually brings more positive actions and events into your life, which eventually start to outweigh the negatives.

CHAPTER 2

DEFINE YOUR VISION

Your visions will become clear only when you can look into your own heart. Who looks outside, dreams; who looks inside, awakes.

—CARL JUNG

The term 'vision' means different things to different people: mission, purpose, dream, and so on. In this chapter, 'vision' refers to your *what* and 'purpose' refers to your *why*: what you want to achieve for yourself and the purpose behind it. Your timeline for achieving your vision could be 12 months, three years, five years, or ten years. Your vision needn't be specific or measurable, especially at first, but to define your vision, consider what you want your future to look like. Close your eyes and imagine how you want to look, act, and feel.

As a young sportsman, I'd envision winning a championship, for example. Outside of straightforward competitions found on a field or in a sports arena, a vision can be ambiguous and difficult to define, or even imagine. This is where The 4 Keys programme can guide you. Think about your business, body, relationships, and mindset, and where you are in regard to each one right now. It's important to take your time and reflect on where you are across The 4 Keys before tackling where you want to go. When you know where you are today and where you want to be, you'll be able to think about how you will get there.

You might focus on how you feel in each key now versus how you want to feel about them in the future. Ask yourself, 'Where am I with my business right now? Where would I like to be? How healthy are my body, my mindset, and my relationships, and where would I like to be with each of these keys at a future time?' The answers to these questions are different for everybody, and no answer is right or wrong if you're being honest with yourself. The most important thing is going through the process, then imagining how you will feel when your vision becomes reality.

Using this technique helps your vision to become a self-fulfilling prophecy. The more you feel it today, the more likely you are to make it happen. Athletes use a similar technique before a game or competition. They visualise competing, the plays they're making, how it feels in the moment, how the coach responds, and even how the spectators are responding. That athlete, even though they are just sitting in their locker room, starts to feel the emotions tied to their imagined actions. Your brain works from a visual perspective, so it doesn't recognise action or inaction. If you can visualise it clearly enough, as far as your brain is concerned, you are in that game. In the same way, when you start to truly feel your vision, you are more likely to make your thoughts become reality.

An athlete who lies awake at night envisioning how they're going to play the next day can feel the physical effects of actually playing. Their heart rate increases, and they become very alert, finding it difficult to fall asleep. Similarly, when you start to envision yourself achieving your vision in any of *The 4 Keys*, whether it's in business, body, relationships, or mindset, you'll begin to experience the physical effects of making your vision a reality.

Having the right mindset and belief for achieving your vision is the difference between winning and losing. Committing to a vision is not about being ruthless or stubborn or about suppressing emotions. It requires openness to change, embracing the unknown, and having absolute belief that you can make your vision a reality. I strongly believe that if you can dream it, you can achieve it. If you think it, you can become it. Your thoughts become a reality, and therefore, you must be careful what you think about. Negative thoughts can become a reality too! On a positive note, if you can visualise what you want, where you want to be, and when you'll achieve it, your thoughts will become a reality. I know this is possible, because I have seen it happen over and over again in my clients.

The biggest challenge you'll face in achieving your vision is believing it's possible to begin with. You'll likely encounter some self-doubt or an internal dialogue that says 'Yeah, but...'. The challenge is not necessarily to ignore these thoughts. You have to learn to get present with them and make sense of your thoughts and the patterns that create them. Then you can shift your thinking in a positive way to the vision of a life that you want for yourself, without hesitation.

When I worked with Team GB, our team vision was actually deluded. We envisioned winning Pool B Gold despite nearly being relegated from Pool B the previous year. I would say to the team, 'I have no doubt in my mind we will win Pool B Gold.' Even though at the time, I didn't know how, the team needed to believe, and that starts with the leader believing in his or her team's potential. There were times when I experienced doubt. My rational mind knew that beating the likes of Austria and Hungary wasn't likely, but we shifted our thinking towards a clear vision and purpose. The biggest game changer for Team

GB Inline Hockey was when one of the players said it wasn't about winning gold. He said, 'When I turn up to Pool B next year, I want to look, act, and feel like a Pool A player.' The gold medal is a clear metric, which is still useful, but the image of turning up like a Pool A team was much more powerful and created a total mindset shift in the players.

I remember one night, after speaking with the team, I returned to the privacy of my hotel room, thinking, *There's no way we're good enough to beat Austria.* Then I reconnected myself with my vision and imagined the feeling of what it would be like to beat Austria. I imagined the cheering faces of my players and the disappointment on the faces of the Austrian players. 'We will beat Austria,' I told myself, and we did. We beat them convincingly, five to one. So even when my team thought I was a little crazy at first, they still had faith in me, and I believed in them, always envisioning us winning the upcoming game. Although we were the underdogs, Team GB wasn't a weak team that relied on belief to get a win. It was strong team of players who used their skills, strategies, and tactics to beat their opponents. But using that vision to create the right mindset gave the players the edge they needed to make it a reality.

When I worked with traders in the city, one of the key factors for their development was to help them look, act, and feel like traders. It was quite a transition for them, as they couldn't see themselves as traders until they were successful and making money. The problem was they would never achieve their goals until they started feeling like successful traders. It is the same for an amateur athlete wanting to become professional. To *become* professional, they have to *feel* like a professional. They have to change their behaviour and act like a professional athlete, which is then more likely to result in a professional contract.

How do you need to feel today to ensure you achieve *your* vision?

Getting into the habit of forming a vision, imagining how it will feel when realised, and having absolute belief in it, whether that's in sports, business, or somewhere else, will help you achieve your objective.

Throughout my business coaching career, I have refrained from using terms like 'law of attraction' and 'self-fulfilling prophecy'. These terms were popularised by the book *The Secret*.[3] I kept it my secret – not that I didn't want people to know about it. I didn't want them to think I'd lost my mind. But the truth is, it works, and I have nothing to be embarrassed about. Team GB and hundreds of business owners, including myself, are a testament. Remember, your thoughts become a reality!

---

3   Rhonda Byrne, *The Secret* (New York: Atria, 2006).

THE 4 KEYS IN ACTION

When I first started helping people define their vision in four keys, I was working with stockbrokers starting their careers in the city. When outlining their visions, they'd talk about flashy cars and having homes in different countries. They were excited by the idea of having total financial freedom – where they could ski all morning, then trade in the afternoon. Their visions were a mix of security, freedom, and materialism.

Shortly after, I was approached by a charity supporting homeless people. The charity had heard about my programme and thought it could be useful in helping their clients get back on their feet, so I agreed to work with them.

In a session with the stockbrokers, each person had to describe how they'd feel if nothing changed from where they are now and if they didn't make it to where they wanted to be. The traders responded with comments such as, 'I'll feel disillusioned,' or 'I'll feel disappointed.' Yes, these are negative words, but not explicitly so, and were what I expected to hear.

During my first session with the charity, however, I was shocked to read what these homeless people had written. I was angry at myself for being naive enough to think I could help these seriously troubled people, and I was emotional, realising the depths of their feelings and the hopelessness of their situations. They wrote, on their 'if nothing changes' Post-it notes, statements like, 'I'll kill myself,' 'I'd jump out of a building,' or 'I'd buy a gun and blow my brains out.' The experience was a stark reality check for me. I could've walked away at that point, but instead, I put on a brave face and said, 'Right, well, this can't happen. We're not going to allow this to happen to you guys. We're going to move forward.' I put the 'if nothing changes' and 'where I want to be' Post-its at opposite ends of the room and instructed the people to walk from the 'now' end to the 'future' end, but they could only take a step if they felt they had everything they needed to make their vision a reality, or if they believed they could achieve their vision. Not one person moved. None of them had any idea where to begin, how to begin, or even thought they could begin.

Eventually, they began talking, trying to find practical solutions to help each other get to their visions. One Hungarian lady said, 'The only thing stopping me is this blob I can see on the floor.' When I asked her what she meant, she said, 'The blob is me. It's as if I'm looking at myself on the floor.' This seemed to resonate with the rest of the group, and they became very animated. This random group of homeless people of all different nationalities began working together. They built a bridge out of chairs and helped her, and each other, over to the other side of the imagined blob. They succeeded in moving forward towards their futures. When you define your vision, remember that you don't go through life alone.

One man wrote, on both of his notes, 'Cleaner'. I began asking him questions like, 'Okay, you're already a cleaner and you want to be a cleaner in the future? Don't you want to build a team of cleaners? Do you want to start your own cleaning business?' He said, 'No. If I've got the same cleaning job in twelve months that I have right now, I'll be in a wonderful place, able to support my wife and children.'

This was a great reminder for me, as a coach, to never force my agenda on someone else. We need to be mindful that not everyone has the same ambition. What might be a limiting belief for me may not be for you. For this guy, he was already good enough in his own mind, but there's still a gap between where he is and where he wants to be – in this case, maintaining his job. He was thankful for his existence, his family, and his job, and that situation brought him peace.

Your vision for each key doesn't have to entail a dramatic change, and in fact, you may be perfectly happy in one or more of your current key places. Your vision will almost certainly be different than another person's because everyone's priorities, values, and situations are different. Don't take this on as a competition. It's a personal experience that only you can do for yourself.

YOUR VISION IN FOUR KEYS

Using *The 4 Keys* to define your vision allows you to compartmentalise each goal by business, body, relationship, or mindset. Think about each one. For some people, putting their thoughts in a journal or on a flipchart makes it easier to define their vision. To create a 'vision board', draw four boxes and label each one as a key. Then draw or write down your initial thoughts for each key. The goal is to identify your what and your why: What do you want your life to look like in 12 months, three years, five years, or whatever time frame you decide, and why?

Before you begin, take 20 minutes to reflect on the following questions in your journal: What is your business like now? How is it performing? Does your business offer you the lifestyle you want? Do you feel good, strong, and powerful in your body? Are you happy with how your body looks? How are your relationships? Are you able to manage your thoughts, feelings, and emotions under pressure? Consider your responses to these questions when you create your vision board. Where do you want to be across your business, body, relationships, and mindset in three to five years – or whatever time frame you choose – from now?

Here's the vision board that I created before starting my business and achieving other objectives in line with *The 4 Keys*. As you can see, it's not particularly detailed or exact, and it's certainly not a work of art. Some of the ideas came about through brainstorming. For example, in my business key, I wanted to connect with one million business owners within five years, so I considered ways to scale, such as creating an online program and writing a book. These seemed like huge tasks when I sketched them on my board, yet I now have an online business, and you are reading my book.

Each picture represents not only a what but a why. For example, in the body key, I want to stay strong so I can ski with my oldest daughter and later with the two youngest, to continue playing hockey on the Vets team, and to play football with my young son. In my relationship key, I am surrounded by my family, and we spend time together at home and while travelling together on holiday. My mindset key represents being calm and at peace with everything around me, yet focused.

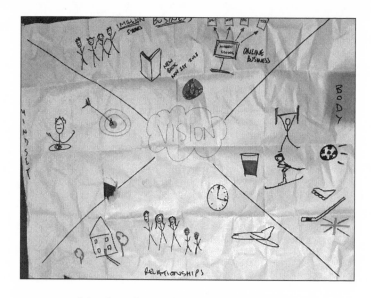

Not surprisingly, when I do this exercise with corporate groups, people with a dominant left brain write numbers and words, while right-brain-dominant people tend to draw their goals. Either is fine. You may find creating a vision board simple, interesting, and fun, or you may find it difficult to visualise your life in the future. Ultimately, it is down to your imagination and not letting your way of thinking hold you back. It's okay to be a little deluded and dream big at this stage.

Now take a moment to think about how you'd feel – in whatever timescale you set for yourself – if nothing changed. Envisioning nothing changing won't feel good if you are seeking change in these facets of your life, and that feeling will reinforce your desire for change and move away from the threat of that happening. Take

LEFT BRAIN AND RIGHT BRAIN

Your brain hemisphere dominance – whether you tend to be a left-brain- or right-brain-typed person – may affect your preferences creating your vision board. If you're having trouble envisioning your future, or if you're unable to enumerate your goals in *The 4 Keys*, don't worry – whether you're a left-brain or right-brain thinker, you can still get where you need to be in your 90-Day Reset. For now, do whatever comes naturally to create your vision board. There is no wrong or right way.

Understanding the differences between left- and right-brain thinkers can also help you better understand the people you interact with at home and at work for improved personal and professional relationships and results.

The two hemispheres have long been the study for neuroscientists and have generated much debate. Due to recent developments in technology, we can now measure brain activity more effectively. There has been a lot of excitement in behavioural and cognitive neuroscience in recent years, and although it may appear as a new discourse in the world of personal and leadership development, there is, however, solid research and science to back up the fact that the two hemispheres have specific functions that are hardwired. Certain skills develop on either the left or right side of the brain and having insight into this will affect how you utilise the strengths in your team.

The left side of the brain is analytical, logical, precise, and time-sensitive. It is particularly good at conceiving and executing complicated plans. It is likely that anyone who has more of a preference for left-brain thinking will prefer planned strategy and a tight framework to avoid any uncertainty. The left side can also be associated with being controlling and unfeeling.

The right brain is associated with being people focused and gentle and tends to be more emotional and at one with the natural world. The right side of the brain likes to dream and empathise. It enjoys creativity and novelty. This type of thinking is likely to generate a desire for an emergent and free-flowing type of strategy.

a moment to write on Post-it notes how you will feel if
nothing happens and you don't achieve your vision.

It may be unpleasant to think about these scenarios,
but accepting them as real possibilities is necessary to
create an urgency to move past a reluctance to change
and create an urgency to change.

Don't get hung up on the negative, though. Get it out there and move on. Establish the time scale, three to five years, or whatever timescale you choose for your vision. It could be ten or even 20 years from now if you want to think that far ahead. Think about what you want your life to look and feel like in that future time. Your vision doesn't need to be granular. You can keep it as high-level as you want at this stage.

If you don't want to write anything at all yet, just think about it. Remember, we will get more pragmatic and results-focused with your 90-Day Reset in Chapter 5.

A VISION FOR YOUR BUSINESS

The greater danger for most of us lies not in setting our aim too high and falling short; but in setting our aim too low and achieving our mark.

—MICHELANGELO

I have spent many days at expensive retreats in Europe, the Middle East, and the United States with businesses facilitating the fine print of their vision statements. I find it fascinating when a business owner asks me to run a vision day for their business. I often hear an owner say, 'Andrew, we'd like you to come in and help us define our vision. Perhaps you could come in for a couple of hours in the afternoon after we have reviewed last year's results in the morning and flesh out what our vision is. Then we plan to go out for a few drinks. You're more than welcome to join us.'

Nothing really gets achieved except for a hangover. Come Monday morning, it is business as usual, apart from the fact the owner has laminated the vision and put it around the office for everyone to ignore.

Whilst away days and team-building days may support aligning your business, I would like you to think more deeply about your personal business vision and what you truly want for you and your family. I would like you to look at where you see yourself now in your career and compare that with where you want to be. Consider the size of your business, the markets you're in, and whether you're local, national, or international. What type of culture do you want to create? What is your role within the business? This is an important question to ask yourself, because a business founder often ends up as CEO as their business grows, and they lose their passion for – and may even come to hate – their business because being CEO doesn't play to their strengths. Now, what do you want your role to be in your future vision?

Slow down and think. Think hard. You're not checking a box here. This is *your* business – how you will be spending many hours every week over a lot of years. Don't focus on what you think other people want from you. Think about what *you* want from you. What is it that you could create with your business, that you would enjoy doing and would really make you proud?

If you like where you are now, keep doing what you're doing. But you don't want to walk into work in five years, thinking, 'Oh no, what have I created?' You'll want to envision a business you look forward to every day, not one you dread. Think about the type of culture you want to create, the people you want to surround yourself with, what it would feel like to create that business and be proud to work in it, lead a team in it, work with clients in it, and talk and write about it.

Take your time and do the work here. By slowing down now, you will be able to move more quickly towards your business key vision in the future.

Take another look at my vision board. You'll see I wasn't thinking about how much money I wanted to make. Instead, I focused on the life I wanted for me, for my team, for my family, and for my clients. I thought about the environment I wanted to create, live, and work in and how I was going to get there. You may have a number in your head – a turnover number you want to hit with your business, and that's fine. But don't lose sight of what's truly important, because that is what makes up the moments that make up the days that make up your life.

A VISION FOR YOUR BODY

All parts of the body which have a function, if used in moderation and exercised in labors in which each is accustomed, become thereby healthy, well developed and age more slowly, but if unused they become liable to disease, defective in growth and age quickly.

—HIPPOCRATES

Your body is how you look and feel. To be the best version of yourself at work and for your family, it's important to take care of your body. There is growing evidence suggesting a positive association between physical activity and psychological well-being – less depression, enhanced cognitive function, and a slowing down in the advancement of dementia and neurocognitive disorder such as Alzheimer's disease. While we shouldn't concentrate too much on vanity, how we look does have an impact on how we feel and vice versa.

When I created my vision board, I didn't focus on developing six-pack abs. I wanted to be strong and healthy so I could enjoy playing sports with my kids and my friends. Thinking about that *why* kept me motivated, whereas if I had focused sheerly on my physical appearance, I may have been caught in a yo-yoing cycle of fat and muscle gain and loss. I have seen this happen with clients, and the reason behind it was clear: they had not done the work of envisioning their what with a powerful enough why to keep them on track.

In your vision, do you feel strong and powerful? Do you feel ready to run, sprint, or lift when you need to? Do you want to compete in some kind of physical contest? Maybe you want to run your first 5K, reduce inflammation in your body, or improve your mobility. Consider your current body and physical self and what you want your body to be like in the future. What will your body be capable of five years from today?

At the risk of sounding cliché, this is a journey and not a destination. Seek to achieve a healthy lifestyle that's enjoyable and sustainable.

According to research, the World Health Organisation (WHO), and government health departments around the world, there are two types of weekly physical activity required to stay healthy: aerobic and resistant. Aerobic, also known as cardio, predominantly means working the lungs and heart and improving the body's ability to utilise oxygen; resistance means mainly contracting the skeletal muscles against gravity or using external weight to enhance muscular strength and endurance. I would also add anaerobic training such as sprints. There is no better way to build strength and get lean than doing several 10- to 20-second sprints once per week combined with the above. If you don't believe me, Google images of sprinters and marathon runners and compare their physiques.

The health choices you make today will have a direct effect on your future health. Perhaps you imagine playing soccer or skiing with your kids when they grow up? In Chapter 6, I will share simple ideas for exercise and nutrition to support your 90-Day Reset.

A VISION FOR YOUR RELATIONSHIPS

If you want to bring happiness to the whole world, go home and love your family.

—MOTHER TERESA

There is no doubt by now – based on your own experiences and what I have openly shared with you about my experience balancing relationships with growing a business – that being an entrepreneur is very tough!

During my time coaching business owners, I have had my fair share of conversations with the spouses too. They share experiences of lonely nights, kids bath times regularly missed, and special moments that can never be shared together again. There is always an excuse – a reason or justification for putting the business first.

The life of an entrepreneur can be a daily grind where it often feels there is no way out, but what about the impact on partners, family, and friends? How do we make time in the day for those we care about who want to be happy and fulfilled too?

Think about how you want your home life to look. What do you see around you, and what sounds do you hear? For example, do you hear your children playing, your wife laughing? How do you make others feel? Maybe you need to strike a better work-life balance, or you want to travel more with your partner, or spend more time with your children. Where do you want to live? What does your home life look like? How does the environment feel?

We seldom use this technique in our personal relationships. It's not a usual practice, and can feel awkward or contrived, but defining a vision around your relationships can be crucial in making sure your goals for all four keys align with one another. My wife and I have struggled to create a joint vision and have had to work very hard at getting aligned. I believe it's where my wife and I disconnected before our separation. It seemed our visions weren't aligned, but in reality, it came down to communication. It fascinates me how much we focus on improving communication in business and sports teams, getting clear on the vision and objectives, and learning about the different personalities within a team to improve business relationships, yet these things are often neglected in the home because there is an expectation that the relationship should work. Once my wife and I worked with a coach, we managed to figure out what was holding us back and have become a cohesive team. This was important to both of us, because even if you're not married, if you have children with a person, the two of you are still in a relationship as parents of those children.

Defining a vision together with your partner is a great test. I recommend it even before marriage to ensure it is aligned. If you're planning to spend the next 30-plus years together, you need to be pulling in the same direction. No matter how attractive you find one another, if you don't share the same goals, you're probably going to struggle in the same way any team would. You need to be brave enough to say it out loud before locking yourselves into a situation that's doomed from the start. This is about planning for the marriage, not planning for the wedding. I'm not a marriage counsellor, but I've seen how unhappy relationships affect people not only in their relationship key but in their other three keys as well.

When it comes to defining your vision in your relationships, ask yourself how you want to experience your relationships. What are you building towards in each relationship with your partner, your family, and your friends? If you're married, what do you want that marriage to feel like? What do you want your relationships with your children to be like? As with all the keys, the investment of time and effort you put in today will pay off in the future. When you have a choice to make between investing in your family or your work, choose your family. The rewards are much greater.

One thing I know for sure, which has been the hardest thing for me to accept – especially with a daughter from a previous relationship – is that your partner is number one, no matter what. You are the king and queen, and you rule your kingdom together with a clear vision for a better future.

It was difficult for me to put someone else before my daughter, but I have learnt the stronger the relationship is with my wife, the stronger the relationship is with Izzie. She appreciates the stability and consistency. My wife must feel like she is number one, and the important hockey game or the night with the boys may need to give if my wife truly needs me and my support. She must trust that I am always there for her. This builds strength and trust in the family and models the right behaviour.

It's been hard to change the pattern that I have inherited

from my father, but that's what sons do. My siblings and I all loved my dad, but we would all agree he was not the best role model when it came to relationships.

You may need to change your pattern to be the best partner and parent. You may have to look deep inside and do the work on yourself to ensure you are being the best version of yourself for others.

A VISION FOR YOUR MINDSET

Do not judge me by my successes, judge me by how many times I fell down and got back up again.

—NELSON MANDELA

Visualise feeling mentally stronger and more confident and able to handle your emotions under pressure. Knowing what to aim for enables you to figure out how to get there. How do you think and feel in that vision? Do you want to feel calmer and more confident? Envision yourself with absolute focus and inner peace. If you look at my vision board, you'll see this is what I strive for, as I'm a firm believer in being focused and able to remain calm under pressure.

Individuals who perform at the highest level have the ability to manage their thoughts, feelings, and emotions. A strong mindset will increase your awareness, clarity of judgment, and decision-making and ability to keep you calm under pressure. These are important strengths for any business leader. There are moments in our life when we act irrationally, and we later reflect on this experience, wondering why it happened. Sound familiar? It is simply a natural response to a perceived threat and what Daniel Goleman refers to as an amygdala hijack in his book *Emotional Intelligence*.[4]

If you don't know what triggers this reaction, you can't anticipate it, and it can happen so fast that you don't have time to respond rationally. The goal is to rationalise the perceived threat and put it into perspective. As mentioned earlier, the brain doesn't differentiate between one threat and another and therefore reacts to stimuli equally, even when the trigger isn't truly threatening. Top performers are able to manage this, remain composed, and maintain clarity during crises. They know that when there is a crisis, there is also an opportunity.

Being self-critical and having high expectations are important components for developing a strong mindset. Although, as a coach I find this can also be one of the most detrimental behaviours in an individual. You have to keep those criticisms and expectations in perspective and manage your thoughts. Whilst being critical of your

---

4   Daniel Goleman, *Emotional Intelligence: Why It Can Matter More Than IQ* (New York: Bantam, 1995).

performance is important, it is also important to know that today you are good enough and tomorrow you can be even better; this is what psychology professor and author Carol Dweck refers to as a 'growth mindset'. Many people don't feel good enough today and lack confidence due to their perception of themselves and old patterns that don't serve them. You probably have a voice in your head that doubts you? This is known as your 'inner critic'.

It's important to get to know your inner critic and become more familiar with the voice inside your head. Most people try to ignore it only to find that it appears when they least expect it. It can cloud your judgment. Just when you realise your goal and strategy, you hear a voice say, 'Yeah but, what if it fails?' The voice can create limiting beliefs and try to throw you off track and prevent you from realising your vision. This is your brain trying to protect you, so it feels counter-intuitive to ignore it or turn it off. All entrepreneurs have an inner critic, but what separates them is their ability to change the tone of that critic to a more helpful voice and then pay attention to it when it serves them and turn down the volume when it does not.

Your inner critic may be a version of you that has been created by the environment you have grown up in. The inner voice is often referred to as the 'gremlin' or a 'bully'. I recommend that you give yours a name. Imagine what it looks like or draw an image of it in your journal. Try and make sense of it. You can also draw a positive image on your vision board. Identify with a useful version: strong, thoughtful – maybe even a spiritual guide and positive advisor, saying what you want and need to hear in the moment and perhaps even showing you a vision of yourself having achieved your mindset key in the future. This level of awareness is essential when working towards your vision and goals. The voice will always be there, so it may as well assist you in reaching your goals rather than preventing you from achievement. Your inner critic may have found its voice in past experiences that you had. While this isn't about therapy, it is about dealing with those things that hold you back, so you can move forward.

Your mindset key is about finding a balance between inner peace, calm, and absolute focus. There are times when you need to act, but you also need to build in time to deal with your inner critic, and anything else that's holding you back. You can do that with meditation or other methods, and they are available to you anyplace and just about any time. In Chapter 7, I'll introduce you to a concept called 'box breathing', inspired by Navy SEAL Mark Divine, who has been using the technique for over 30 years. My clients have found this method incredibly useful for improving their emotions under pressure.

YOUR KEY OUTCOMES ARE LIMITED ONLY BY YOUR VISION

Right now, don't worry about *how* you're going to do any of these things, and don't limit yourself by questioning the possibilities. Nothing is too crazy or outlandish, so write it all down. I have seen so many business leaders realise their full potential and lead the life they imagined by starting with this simple vision exercise. It is a very powerful way to get you into action, living the life you should be living.

The best business leaders I have worked with encourage their entire team to believe in them and their shared vision. That belief lets them set aside those nagging doubts like, 'The market is too competitive. We're too small, there's no way we can compete in this market. We'll never have the home we want or the lifestyle we dream of.' But you will. I have no doubt you'll make your dreams a reality, because I have experienced it and seen it over and over again. There is no magic dust to making it happen. It will take commitment and absolute belief.

If your vision seems too big and overwhelming, keep in mind that you will be developing a 90-Day Reset which will enable you to take a pragmatic approach to making it happen. But also bear in mind that you won't be relentlessly doing this day to day, back to back, which can result in burnout. You'll make sustainable improvements within each 90-Day Reset that you can easily maintain between plans, when you'll be resting and getting back to your usual life, only closer to your vision. Downtime is just as important as the game plan itself.

You may feel like you're getting out of your comfort zone during the 90-Day Reset. You will be pushing yourself but in a way that protects you from burnout and allows you to make dramatic changes in all four keys of your life. Your vision board may start off as a bunch of images on paper, but they represent real possibilities that you can and will achieve when you are willing to stretch yourself just a little further.

If you haven't drawn a vision board yet, do it now. If you have some Post-it notes handy, start writing down ideas. If you keep a journal, start listing them there. Don't put this off. Put it on paper right now.

EXERCISE: WRITE A POSTCARD TO YOURSELF FROM THE FUTURE

You've explored your current position and found out what it is you're not happy with. You created your vision board, dreaming big across *The 4 Keys* for your future vision, and you've mounted this on your wall. Now take a postcard and write it from the you of the future – the one who has achieved the visions on your vision board – whether they're three months, six months, or five years in the future. Write the card to the current you, telling yourself how it feels to be where you are, having achieved your vision. Once you've written your postcard, take a step back and think about what you need to do to get to that future point. What did the future you do to get there? What did it take? What sort of changes did you make across your four keys to achieve that life? This is a simple but illuminating exercise that provokes real thought and insight.

Here's an example of a postcard from a future self:

> *1 October 2022. You would so want to be here right now! We have an apartment in Prague, and we decided to head to the Czech mountains. I'm looking out at the mountains right now. I took a walk before breakfast and am feeling fitter and stronger than ever. It's so wonderful to have everyone here together. Izzie has a great career and is thriving; we went on a hike together yesterday. I spent the afternoon playing ball with Harry and Freya, and tonight is my favourite night of the week – date night with my wife. Lucie's business has really taken off and is thriving. Oh, and Get Fit To Win has made a difference to over one million business leaders worldwide. We have a Get Fit To Win conference planned next month to celebrate the success. Anyway, wish you were here.*
>
> *P.S. When are you getting here?*

The point of this exercise is to get clearer about your purpose and to prompt you to think about how you're going to connect your current self to your future self. Keep the postcard simple by breaking it down into four easy steps.

Step 1: Set yourself an imaginary future date from which you'll be writing your postcard.

Step 2: Describe the achievements under the headers on your vision board, such as business growth, your role, weight loss, and so on.

Step 3: Write the postcard from your future self. Make sure you include words that describe what you see, hear, and feel. This is your untold story that hasn't come to pass yet, so make sure you describe your emotions and your achievements too.

Step 4: From your future point of view, look back at the steps you had to take to get to this point. What were the key events, decisions, and challenges you faced? How did you overcome the hurdles? What type of mindset did you have to adopt to achieve this vision? This is a good time to consider the non-urgent projects and tasks that you seem to put off because you're busy with whatever needs to be done at the moment. These non-urgent activities are critical to your progress and will make the greatest difference in your future. Write down some of your non-urgent tasks. You'll revisit these later when you're designing your 90-Day Reset, but you should write them down now, while you're envisioning your future.

CHAPTER 3

——

KNOW YOUR WHY

He who has a why can bear almost any how.

—FRIEDRICH NIETZSCHE

Before we dive into how to turn your vision into reality, it's vital that you understand your motivation, commonly known as your 'why'. At this point, you know where you want to go. Now you have to figure out why you want to get there. A person may have a goal such as, 'My vision is to have a six pack.' But when that person is challenged to explain the reason behind that goal, it may never be strong enough to act as real motivation. You may have to go deeper. For example, I don't want to have inflammation in my body, because I want to be active, participate in sports, and play with my children. I don't want to be in pain. So my reason behind the visions is a desire to be healthy, inspire others to take care of their own health, and to be there for my children. Sometimes, when staying motivated to train or making better food choices is difficult, I think of my mastermind group. The Get Fit To Win Mastermind is a group of elite entrepreneurs and business leaders who challenge, support, and hold each other accountable. I think about how they need me to inspire them, which in turn inspires me to keep going and push harder. Another strong motivator is the desire to thrive with my family and to be playful with them.

Your why may be born out of your past stories and experiences that have shaped you. These could be positive or traumatic ones. Either way, they are powerful. For me, my dad's life and his death have influenced my why. Friedrich Nietzsche said, 'He who has a why can bear almost any how,' and it's true. A strong why is a powerful motivator. Simon Sinek talks about Apple's why. But I believe that's not strictly accurate. It's not Apple's why, it's Steve Jobs' why. It is very hard, if not impossible, to get a unified team why because it's too personal. What made Apple, *Apple* was Steve Jobs' refusal to compromise on his why. If you weren't willing to 'think differently, challenge the status quo', and build beautiful machines, you wouldn't be working with him for long.

Employees have their own whys that vary wildly from the organisational ones. For example, a young guy may say that what gets him out of bed every day isn't the pay cheque he's bringing home for himself but for his family.

He comes from a poor background, and now he's working in a sales environment and making good money. What drives him to action every day is the opportunity to give his family a good, comfortable, safe life.

Remember that the people on your team don't, and often won't, have the same why as you, but you can have work visions that align with one another. As a business owner, your challenge is to align your team's whys and visions, so what they want supports the company's vision and working towards it satisfies their why. Your other responsibility is being willing to emotionally engage with your own why and being vulnerable and open enough with your team to act as a role model for their own alignment. It takes bravery to stand up and say to your team, 'This is my why' and 'This is my vision and the vision we're working towards.'

Anita Roddick of Body Shop, referred to as the 'capitalist with a conscience', understood the fine balance between having a strong why and a marketing message. She managed to build a whole business around this and built a team that shared her vision of standing against animal testing.[5] Like Simon Sinek says, people don't buy what you do, they buy why you do it. Your why has to be more than just a marketing ploy. As a leader, people will con-

5   'Anita Roddick, Capitalist with a Conscience, Dies at 64', *The Independent*, September 11, 2007, accessed September 15, 2018, https://www.independent.co.uk/news/uk/this-britain/anita-roddick-capitalist-with-a-conscience-dies-at-64-402014.html.

nect with you or buy from you because of your ability to emotionally connect them to your offering. They don't care that you're the CEO or the business owner, but they *do* care what you stand for. Your why has to be real and genuine, not contrived. And then, when you're growing your business, you know you've got the right people joining you, because they're able to align their personal why to your vision. You and your employees need to believe in, and hold on to, the overarching company vision.

Trying to appease everyone will never work. It'll simply dilute your purpose and end in dissatisfaction, so build a diverse team of talented individuals who will challenge you in the right way but who can fit their personal visions and purpose into your company vision.

PASSION VS. PURPOSE

There's a difference between passion and purpose. Passion is what we love. For example, I'm passionate about roller hockey. I love it. Passion is what serves us. Purpose, on the other hand, is about serving others. Your purpose becomes your why. How do you, through your purpose, serve others? Your customers? Your team? Your friends and family? From this identification of purpose, your values begin to manifest.

What is your motivation for change? Why is it important

to you? Who, besides yourself, will benefit from these changes? Answering these questions encourages you to think outside of yourself. Why did you create your vision? Why is the postcard from the future important to you? Who else benefits from that future?

When I spoke to young hockey players, I told them how much I loved the game. I played and practised every day. I always wanted to win. I wanted to be the best. I would get quite upset and frustrated when, particularly at men's world level, other players would go out drinking at the world championships. They'd say, 'We're away for ten days. We've got to relax and have fun.' I would be thinking, *We're away for ten days to play hockey, not to go out and drink.* Then they'd turn up for a match the next day hung over, and I'd be so angry. On reflection, this was selfish of me because I was only serving myself by fulfilling my passion. However, if you play with purpose, you're still playing with intent, but you're playing with the intent to make the rest of the players better. For me, this is at the very heart of leadership.

Like many other young players, in my early playing days, it was all about proving myself to the coach, Mark Cavallin, and holding on to the puck a bit longer to try and beat more players or pull off a fancy play. I was a selfish player. At one point, I apologised to my coach for not scoring goals, and he told me to stop trying. He told me to instead focus on assisting other players and letting them score the goals. Suddenly, through this selfless play, I started scoring more goals. Mark led the team with purpose. He was more concerned with developing and teaching us as individuals and not just players, and his consistency and sense of purpose made me really trust him.

The same principles of selflessness and serving others can be applied to business. The best way to get out of your own head is to serve other people. Move the puck quicker and give other players more time on the puck. You're stronger when you're serving others and when you're working as part of a unit, so dare to let go and allow others to thrive so they can realise their visions as well.

ALIGN YOUR WHY ACROSS THE 4 KEYS

It's easier to find the purpose for your business than for your relationships because the purpose for a business tends to be more pragmatic, although it may border on marketing messages. While they may have value, business whys can distract from the deeper, more meaningful whys that transcend across all four keys.

My why has often been about helping people create an environment in which they can thrive, feel inspired, and reach their full potential. This translates into helping them become fit and healthy with a positive mindset. I did this with Team GB and with businesses and executives.

However, I didn't think about the environment I was creating at home. I wasn't present for my wife or children. For example, I'd never look at my phone halfway through a client meeting, but it never occurred to me that looking at texts and email messages during dinner with my family was just as wrong.

Once I took a deeper look at my purpose – *I get up in the morning to help others thrive* – I realised my why shouldn't be limited to my professional life. Paying the bills may be an immediate priority, but it meant very little in the long run, especially compared to other priorities, like my children. Tapping into that why and applying it to my relationships was incredibly important. When I could do that, I connected better with my family, and this reflected back across my business by making me a better coach and team leader.

Each of *The 4 Keys* is linked. Business. Body. Relationships. Mindset. When something impacts one key, the effects are felt across all four, whether the influence is positive or negative. If your business suffers, so do your relationships. If your health improves, so does your mindset. If your mindset improves, so do your relationships.

HOLD YOURSELF ACCOUNTABLE

Professionally, you're held accountable. You have a boss or a manager, and you have a team and clients who have certain expectations. If you need help to remain accountable with your physical health, you can hire a personal trainer. You can even take a mindfulness course.

Have you ever taken a relationship course? Or a class on how to be a better partner or parent? One reason my Get Fit To Win Mastermind is so effective is there's nowhere to hide. You put your visions out there for the whole group to see, and they hold you accountable. When you join *The 4 Keys* programme or subscribe to its mastermind community, you'll find someone who can help you and who will act as your accountability coach.

With your closest relationships, this level of dispassionate accountability is more difficult to attain because there are intense emotions involved. Even if you're in a mature, stable relationship, it's difficult to sit down and hear from your partner that they didn't like the way you spoke to them and to not react negatively or even become defensive to that. The dynamic is completely different from a professional situation. With a colleague or a client, you'd likely say, 'Okay, I'm sorry about that. Let's sit and talk it through,' but in your personal relationships, it's not that simple. Unless you can look outside yourself, it's likely you'll feel affronted, like your partner doesn't support you or your vision.

Writing this now sounds absolutely ridiculous, but one day, I'd been looking forward to an apple crumble my mum had made. (My mum makes the best apple crumble!) I got home, and my wife and daughter had eaten it all. I'm embarrassed to say that I was instantly, irrationally furious. I literally had a tantrum. I remember yelling, 'Do you realise how hard I work? And you ate all the crumble.' It sounds ridiculous now, but at the time I blew my lid and felt rightfully justified doing so. In hindsight, I can see I was ignoring *The 4 Keys* and was only thinking about myself. Yes, I was going out and making money, but I wasn't listening to my family or truly serving them, and they were more than entitled to all of it.

This is why holding yourself accountable is so important. Respect the people in your life enough to face them, to be present with them, and to seek to understand them. Back then, when faced with a situation such as this, I may have said, 'Why don't you respect me?' Now I would say to myself, and I would suggest to anyone experiencing the same situation, 'What am I doing or not doing that's causing my family not to respect me?' We have to look at ourselves and ask, 'What's going on here?' Then we'll have that epiphany where we realise we're on autopilot, taking our families for granted and assuming they'll love and respect us just because we work hard.

YOUR STORIES SHAPE YOU

In 2014 I was hired to coach a team of about 17 people in the Middle East, and a man named Ajay was the team leader. My first task was getting everyone on the team to open up to one another. It was a cultural melting pot of a team, with Palestinians, Swedes, Germans, English, Americans, and Jordanians. I told Ajay that I had an exercise that would be useful to get people to start talking, but he said, 'No, no, no. I've got *this* exercise. I'll start by talking about my family, and we'll all do it, one by one.' He stood up and reeled off facts about his family, like he's got two children, a wife, and so on. All 17 of them then did this in turn, and I did it too. It was incredibly awkward and impersonal. The exercise fell flat, and I went on to do the day's team coaching.

Then we did a psychometric evaluation with Ajay and all the members of the team to try and learn more about each other. Later, I had to meet Ajay in an Istanbul hotel to go through his psychometric results and the feedback from his team, moving this to an executive coaching role. Ajay hadn't booked a meeting room, so he upgraded his hotel room to a suite, and the two of us sat in his suite and went through the feedback, none of which was new or surprising. Ajay was a seasoned team leader, and I thought the conversation would go nowhere. This was before my TEDx Talk, so I'd never really opened up with a coaching client, but in an impromptu moment, I said, 'Ajay, let me explain why I do what I do.'

I told him about my dad, and as I finished, Ajay looked down at his feet. I knew it was random to sit in a Turkish hotel suite, telling a client who I had formed a good relationship with this personal story about my dad. During an awkward silence, I thought Ajay might be thinking it was inappropriate. He went very quiet. Then he told me about *his* father and why perfection, resilience, and working hard were so important to him.

Ajay's father migrated during India Partition and survived the genocide. He was forced to hide beneath a pile of dead bodies until the mass killings stopped. He managed to escape across the border, where he met his wife. As Ajay talked, he started to cry, then said, 'Andrew, I don't do this. I don't cry.' He left the room for the bathroom. When he returned, I told him that he *had* to tell his team this story. They needed to hear more than dry facts, and they needed to see behind this polished exterior of the man who pushed them to complete their work without ever making a personal connection with any of them.

I coached and prepped him, helping him relate the

extraordinary tale in a real way that let him express the depth of emotion and let his audience connect with it. Once he voiced his story to the team, the dynamics changed. They changed completely. There had been distance and a degree of uncertainty from his team, but on hearing why he strived so hard for perfection, why he behaved a certain way, and why delivering brilliant service was so important, they understood him and bought into him.

It took me six months, two trips to Dubai, and two trips to Turkey, but I eventually got all 17 team members to share their own stories, passions, and motivations.

Getting clear on the stories that shaped you and *how* they shaped you is crucial for business leaders because it helps others understand you, connect with you, and ultimately, believe in you. Stories still deliver data and facts, but they do it in a deeper, more meaningful way. Our stories make sense of what we have become as we can make the necessary changes that will have a positive impact on our lives and the lives of those around us. By doing so, you'll experience a shift in how people respond to you.

For example, I have noticed a direct correlation between improved client engagement and my TEDx Talk. The best talk I ever gave happened when the technology wasn't working, so I couldn't show my 10 slides. I had to describe them through storytelling. Now I never use slides. I just tell the story, and people connect with it.

FIND STRENGTH IN VULNERABILITY

Vulnerability is not a sign of weakness but a source of power. To be a great leader, you must show humility and vulnerability. To the contrary, it's the mask you're wearing that's your weakness. Vulnerability is about being completely open – being metaphorically naked. Think about that infamous dream where you go to work, to a networking event, or to another public event and you look down and realise you're naked. Imagine being so at ease with who you are that you could just walk anywhere, totally open and metaphorically naked, shaking hands and making meaningful connections.

In Lewis Howes' *The Mask of Masculinity*, the author describes 'nine common masks of masculinity that men wear interchangeably'.[6] I recommend this book to anyone who wants to learn more about how men use these masks to deal with their insecurities and avoid being truly vulnerable. Women may also appreciate the book as a guide to the masks their male colleagues or partners may be wearing so they can better understand them.

---

6 Lewis Howes, *The Mask of Masculinity: How Men Can Embrace Vulnerability, Create Strong Relationships, and Live Their Fullest Lives* (Emmaus: Rodale, 2017).

Being vulnerable and humble also gives you authenticity that's impossible to replicate. It makes you real and relatable and lends natural gravitas and presence without contrived or ostentatious gravitas or presence. It's about being who you are and believing other people will accept you that way. This authenticity and presence make people say, 'He's just got an aura about him.'

Think back to the cleaner – so at ease with who he was and content with what he had. Sometimes there's conflict between ambition and tension, 90-day plans, and the realisation that some things are good enough. You don't need to drive forward and make monumental changes in all four keys all the time. The plan doesn't need to be perfect; it just needs to move you forward. We are genetically hardwired to keep moving forward, to keep exploring and embracing change. It has aided human survival for the last two million years.

EXERCISE: FIND YOUR SUPERPOWER

Think about Ajay and his superpower. His drive for perfection and organisation made him a successful team leader and his father's plight shaped him.

What are your strengths? What do you bring to the business? What's your superpower, and what are the stories that shaped you and created your superpower?

How are those stories shaping you today? What's your story?

Think of your stories, the ones that spark emotions in you. Think about your good and bad experiences. Are they helping you or holding you back? How can you turn them into something that will serve you and others? Have these stories moulded patterns in your behaviour? Do you need to change the pattern?

Everyone has a story. You may feel a bit narcissistic, writing your story, but you will find clues to your current behaviours, patterns, and your superpower in it, and telling your story is a powerful way to communicate your journey to others. If you watch a TED Talk, you'll see that every speech is simply data wrapped in a story. If the presenters came on stage and shared PowerPoint slides filled with data, do you think the audience would be as engaged? Do you think the presenter would be able to connect with the audience or that the audience would even understand or remember the message?

Everyone has a story. Why not have a go at writing yours and sharing it with someone? You can write it out and share it that way or practise presenting it verbally. If you're not accustomed to speaking publicly, consider joining Toastmasters or another public speaking group. There is power in stories, and your superpower is buried in your story. Write your story. Find your superpower. Then share your superpower by telling your story to others.

CHAPTER 4

———

FIRM YOUR FOUNDATION

Your beliefs become your thoughts,
Your thoughts become your words,
Your words become your actions,
Your actions become your habits,
Your habits become your values,
Your values become your destiny.

—GANDHI

Whatever you're doing or creating, you need a firm foundation on which to build something that lasts. If you build your house on sand, it'll be unstable and unsustainable as the sand erodes from beneath it.

Businesses often establish values, but if they don't reflect the company and its people, they're merely marketing jargon or words on a wall. When you define your own core values or those of your business, you will need to dig deep and really think about the kind of person you want to be – what you want to stand for. Envision your future self, perhaps a year from today, and where you and your business will be if you begin to live your core values today.

Working with Team GB, I took a clinical, pragmatic approach to values. I introduced a set of core values to the locker room and witnessed a genuine shift in behaviour. Furthermore, there was an obvious connection between the behavioural change and the results we achieved. This dramatic shift made everyone feel safe in the locker room – even guys who fought like cats and dogs every week. Having those values gave them common ground.

Because it worked so well for the team, I began to question my own values as a human being. I realised that sometimes we hold on to values that work against us, often subconsciously. For example, when I was a kid, I'd always look for the easiest route, or I'd not do my work, then try to make up excuses. That subconscious value left over from school of always looking for the easiest way was not helpful. It was destructive and limiting. I had to make a conscious effort to replace it with something that does serve me, such as, 'Give every task 100 per cent of my effort, and never make excuses.'

My mum was an extremely optimistic person, and she encouraged me to pursue my dreams and play hockey. She instilled many values in me that later enabled me to be more resilient. However, she also let me do almost anything I wanted, and she didn't pressure me to do things that I didn't want to do. For example, if I didn't want to go to school, I had nobody to tell me, 'It's not about whether or not you want to go, it's about resilience, commitment, and long-term gain,' so I was allowed to be lazy without correction. My dad was also very laid back, and while their relaxed parenting encouraged me to be a free thinker, which I am grateful for, it didn't teach me the accountability, responsibility, or any other core values that every child needs.

This is another example of how past experiences shape us, and not always for the better. Because of my lack of parental discipline, now I make a concerted effort to instil the right values in my daughter. I help her develop a work ethic by letting her know she *has* to do the work. I instil in her that it's not okay to make excuses or lie, and that she must be honest and speak the truth about the way she feels. I don't just preach at her, however. I make an effort to be a role model for her, practising these values in all aspects of my life so she has a clear example to follow. Legacy isn't just about what you leave behind financially; legacy is about the values you leave behind for future generations to live by.

GET FIT TO WIN FOUNDATIONS

Like a sturdy structure, the 90-Day Reset has a clear set of values which I refer to as the Foundations. They underpin everything we do at Get Fit To Win, and you can use them to guide your decisions and create sound, meaningful, sustainable change.

1. Do the Work.
2. No Excuses.
3. Always Ready.
4. Speak the Truth.

Simple, right? Implementing these foundations seems easy, but if the stories that shaped you don't reflect them, you may have to make a conscious effort to instil the foundations into your current everyday behaviour. For some of us, the Foundations are ambitions we aim to live by, even though we may fail from time to time. Let's discuss each one in detail.

DO THE WORK

This first foundation requires you to take action. Words and thoughts are meaningless unless you act on them. The plan you'll have at the end of this book – your vision – is just words on paper until you *do the work*.

If you want to succeed across *The 4 Keys*, you have to do

the work. It's all too easy, particularly when you start your 90-Day Reset, to let yourself get distracted by whatever's the easiest to work on. It is essential that you stay focused and direct your energy into working on everything that's relevant to your vision, however difficult. Remember that doing the work is much easier when you've got a strong why because that is a strong motivator tied to your vision.

Your brain is designed to keep you safe, but feeling safe can be counteractive. Getting outside your comfort zone is when change happens, but your brain, in trying to keep you safe, encourages you to stay firmly inside that comfort zone. It will tell you that you don't need to work out today, that you don't want to get up early, that you want to stay safe and warm, tucked up in bed. You need to take action that pushes you out of that safe zone. Start with little things like putting your alarm clock over the other side of the room so you *have* to get out of bed. Remind yourself that what your brain is doing to keep you safe is not serving you. It's working against you, keeping you from achieving your vision. You may, of course, be on the other extreme: a person who always feels pressed to act and can never slow down. If this describes you, then you may need to build time into your schedule to relax.

Doing the work is about getting uncomfortable, but it's not about overexertion. You will create a wider comfort zone by working smarter to get outside of your existing comfort zone, taking actions over and over that make you a little uncomfortable until your safe zone grows to incorporate those actions.

Start small. Choose something that will benefit you in the long run. For example, for your body key, commit to sweating a little every day, maybe block out 20 to 30 minutes daily to get your heart rate up. You might run a mile, pedal for 15 minutes on an exercise bike, or go for a walk in the neighbourhood park. Do it every single day for 21 days – the number of days it takes to create a habit. You could also make an adjustment to your diet, such as giving up sugar for 21 days. The foundations are not limited to the body key. Winning in your business, relationships, and mindset requires you do the work. While you might not want to at first because it's outside the 'safe' zone, hold to your values and your whys, and power through. Eventually, you will have created new pathways in your brain, and this physical activity or eating habit that you found so hard at first will become effortless and part of your regular routine.

NO EXCUSES

The *no excuses* foundation was inspired by my mentor, Jock. We trained in his garage, a 'gym' of sorts with these rusty old weights. The whole thing was very *Rocky*-esque. Jock taught me that the only thing that limited me was me, and he helped me understand what I was capable of achieving. He had this innate ability to inspire and motivate. It was Jock who first introduced me to the idea of the inner voice and how much it holds us back, and this has continued to be hugely influential for me.

I was 17 and really argumentative. I'd argue with anyone – my friends, my team – everyone. Jock first gave me the book *How to Win Friends and Influence People*, then *How to Stop Worrying and Start Living*. These simple books changed my life. Reading these and taking action on them changed how I approached situations and conversations. Jock inspired me to move into coaching. Jock taught me that ego was irrelevant. He instilled in me that it didn't matter what you wore, how big you were, or how much you lifted. He didn't care about those things. What mattered was that you worked the hardest and tried your absolute best without making excuses. It is the same in my Get Fit To Win Mastermind group. It doesn't matter how much your business makes, what you drive, or the watch you wear. There is no bravado or showing off. What matters is that you do the work. Everyone does the work, and no one makes excuses.

In his rough, dirty old garage, Jock had my friends and I doing CrossFit-style workouts in the early '90s before CrossFit was even a thing. We did high-intensity interval training with constant movement. Sometimes we sprinted and carried each other up hills. It was about moving our bodies. It was very primal, probably why I am such an advocate of the primal movement and why I follow a primal nutrition and fitness lifestyle. If he'd still been alive, Jock would've adored CrossFit, but he sadly passed away in 2012 after valiantly battling a brain tumour, meningitis, and eventually dementia. He fought to the end, even still going to the gym, so he will always be my inspiration for doing the work and never making excuses.

Everyone at Jock's funeral had a story to share about how he had inspired them, but it was so personal that everyone felt they were the only one he had helped. If I had half the impact on the people I coach that Jock had on the people around him, I would consider myself an enormously successful person and coach. Even now, when I go to the gym and my negative inner voice tries to speak up, Jock's voice is in there, spurring me on.

ALWAYS READY

The *always ready* foundation is about being properly prepared mentally, physically, and in any other way required to meet your obligations and any action you need to take to make progress in *The 4 Keys*. This means thinking ahead to what's coming and making decisions that set you up for success.

IT'S NOT ABOUT WORK-LIFE BALANCE...
IT'S ABOUT DOING THE WORK

If you're striving for work-life balance day to day, then you're probably getting frustrated, disappointed, and annoyed. Instead of trying to balance your life evenly, consider taking a different approach.

Do the Work + No Excuses.

If you want to be healthy, strong, and fit for life, but don't have time due to your busy schedule, then it's likely to be down to the choices you make. Haven't got time for a 10-minute HIIT session in your hotel room? Not able to choose a healthy food option over unhealthy ones?

No Excuses.

No time for your partner and children because you're working late? Are you being as productive as possible, or are you truly maxed out? If the latter, then get proactive and book something for the weekend. Give your spouse time out. Get a date night in the diary.

Do the Work.

If your head is feeling fried from the lack of 'headspace', then book time to practise a little deep breathing or 'box breathing'. Take a walk, leave the smartphone in the office for 15 minutes.

These choices have a direct impact on your mindset, mental toughness, and well-being.

Forget work-life balance. Get up and do the work *daily* – no excuses.

For example, I suffer from chronic arthritis, but I don't let that keep me from playing hockey or being active. When I identified the triggers that caused me pain, I took actions to eliminate them. Eating grains, consuming too much sugar, and eating unhealthy fats were obvious culprits, and so I had to avoid these inflammatory triggers, especially the day before I was going to be playing.

Identifying the triggers that harm you rather than help you makes you more mindful and ensures you can start making better decisions. In my case, I had to make better nutritional choices for my body key.

In regard to your business key, you want to be ready to start each day strong, so you have to be aware of the choices you make the day prior around nutrition, sleep, and any preparations you need to make. You also need to ensure your mindset key is sharp, so you can be your best for the people with whom you interact, both personally and professionally.

You also have to always be ready to be with your children. Are you ready to get the kids in the car, ready to take them to the park, ready to play football with them? Do you feel powerful? Do you feel strong? Are you mentally ready to spend several hours enjoying your family? These questions should drive the choices you make every day.

You don't need to concern yourself with natural selection. You can leave the house without worrying about being preyed on or needing to be fit to hunt. You can eat what you like, exercise very little, and still survive and reproduce. Your ancestors were always ready. They were mindful. They knew a small graze could become infected and cause death. Taking on the always ready approach is about being mindful, thinking ahead. This also means not overextending or overexerting yourself, so that you always have something left in the tank when you need it. Your ancestors wouldn't do something that put their health at risk and prevented them from moving fast and neither should you.

The always ready foundation often incorporates fuel. If you want to be mentally and physically ready and able, you have to fuel your body properly. Find a nutritional plan that works for you and is sustainable. Try to view food as fuel and remember that you want to put the best possible fuel in your body to help your physical and cognitive capabilities.

I know if I make the wrong nutrition choices, I'm going to have an arthritis or gout flareup, or I'm going to feel rough and not be able to be the best version of myself. If I don't go out and train or go to the gym, or if I'm not following through on my commitment to sweat a little every day, or in some cases, I overtrain and don't allow my body to rest, my choices can cause a fight-or-flight response, elevating cortisol levels and reversing the effects of training. Rather than feeling energised from a workout, the chronic training makes me want to sleep and binge on the most convenient and available food.

Take a simple, mindful approach to being mentally and physically ready. It's okay to 'cheat' on occasion, as long as you're aware of that and not failing all the time.

As I mentioned, I inherited gout from my dad. One time, a client invited me and my team out for beers. I knew I'd regret it the next day, and I thought about going but not drinking. We were celebrating coming to the end of a successful six-month collaboration, so I wanted to enjoy the party with everyone, so in the end, I did go, and I had a beer, but I didn't overdo it. I suffered a little the next day, but it wasn't horrendous, and I got right back into my routine.

Always ready doesn't mean being so strict and hard on yourself that you can't enjoy life. Maybe you get together with your friends and enjoy a beer or eat some junk food. I recommend the 80/20 rule in favour of healthy living, but don't aim for 80 per cent, aim for 100 per cent and you're more likely to maintain the 80/20 rule. Always ready is about being mindful so when you do have a few beers, enjoy them and appreciate them!

Always ready is about taking time out to relax and

recharge. People in the Get Fit To Win Mastermind have benefitted from yoga, meditation, and mindfulness. They integrate breathing techniques (which I'll discuss in Chapter 7) to improve their health, well-being, and performance. It's not about being constantly tense and ready to react; it's being present with the world around you and prepared for whatever comes next.

Remember that none of us is perfect and that we're all works in progress. It's okay if you don't manage to live by your values 100 per cent of the time, every single day. There *will* be times when you don't manage it, but as long as you get back on your path, you'll make progress. Just get back in the game and focus on what will get you to your vision faster.

SPEAK THE TRUTH

Being the best version of yourself means speaking the truth to yourself and to others and not sugar-coating things. As an adult, I've learnt to be brave, open to facing the truth, and willing to act on it appropriately. I've had to tell the truth. Be honest about what you want, remembering sometimes you have to be a little self-serving to serve others.

You don't need to tell everybody you meet your deepest, darkest secrets, nor do you have to tell someone the stark, unadorned truth and hurt them without cause. But you need to be honest about what you want, and you need to face the truth when it's in front of you.

In the past, I've used hockey to avoid facing situations I should have been dealing with. People have said to me, 'You love hockey so much, and you're so passionate about it.' Yes, I am, because when I play hockey, I lose myself in the game to the exclusion of all else.

The same thing applied to me when I was younger, regarding relationships. I would choose a dysfunctional relationship over not being in a relationship. The Friday before my dad died, I told my friend Zoe what a great, open relationship I had with my dad and that I was very lucky. It wasn't until I said it out loud that I realised the truth in those sentiments. I really did love him and care about him. Sadly, he passed away two days later. A week later, Zoe came to see me, and our relationship suddenly became serious very quickly without any time to truly grieve by myself. I genuinely cared about her, but I do believe I used the relationship as a distraction to shield me from the grief I was feeling, the pain I didn't want to face. In hindsight, I should have found a proper way to grieve my father. Not being in a relationship left me alone to face my feelings, and it hurt. But that introspective time is crucial. I just didn't know it at the time. Unfortunately, that pattern continued for a while, and

I continued to use relationships to avoid dealing with the truth.

At the time of writing, it's been 25 years since my dad died, and it's taken me this long to recognise that my obsession with hockey – as well as my clinging to relationships that weren't really the best fit for me – was detrimental in the end and that I needed to grieve. But thanks to the foundations – particularly, always speak the truth – I was able to face my truth and overcome my obsession with hockey. My dad's obsession was alcohol. He would say that he wasn't an alcoholic and that beer was his medicine. Those beers were his way of dealing with his demons, and hockey was mine – hockey and relationships.

We all have things we cling to or habits that help us in the short term, but which may not enable us to be the best version of ourselves. Are there habits, patterns, or behaviours that you are clinging onto that may not be serving you or those around you?

A few years ago, I went to my sister's cabin in the Alps. There's no TV and no Wi-Fi – just me and the quiet. I first felt like I was going insane, but I came out of it feeling great. It was like a silent retreat. I'd go for a run up in the mountains and maybe nod good morning to someone, but there were no other distractions, so I had plenty of time to deal with my thoughts and feelings. I got present with my feelings, which allowed me to become mindful of them rather than just saying, 'I'm feeling this, and I don't like it, so I'm going to go play hockey or go hang out with this person.' Instead of avoidance, removing distractions and becoming present allows you to look at a feeling, root out what's causing it, and move on in a healthy way. I have learnt how to be present with my feelings. This is not natural for men – to take time out and sit mindfully and notice our feelings. Our ancestors did this all the time, and it is hardwired in us to find a quiet time to think and reflect. It's important that you build time in for you so you can be your best self for others.

So what are you doing over and over again that isn't serving you? Are you present in your relationships with your partner, parents, and children? Or are you in a relationship with the relationship (like I was, over and over again) rather than the other people in it?

Becoming more present in your relationships begins with empathy, feeling what others are feeling. Experiencing yourself through their eyes can help you better understand how your actions affect other people.

Maybe you don't want to experience empathy or feel a certain way because it makes you uncomfortable or takes you to an emotionally dangerous place. Perhaps you react by drawing away and shutting down. For a long time, I was not able to hug my mum. Can you believe that? Not being able to hug your own mum? I would freeze. Not just my mum either. I responded to anyone this way when they were upset. Those feelings took me back to that evening with my dad and the terrified feeling I had in my dream, and I wanted to avoid that. People need you to empathise with them, and you have to find the strength to empathise with them and be able to console them.

I'm a prime example of the fact that you don't have to be a mindless product of your upbringing. You can take the best bits and deliberately turn your back on the things that don't serve you, like learnt laziness. All you need to do is to get a little introspective.

Those are some of my truths. Now it's your turn. Look inside yourself and identify which things don't benefit you or which hold you back. Examine all your subconscious values and ask yourself what they mean for you. Will they help you achieve your vision or slow you down? How are they helping or hindering you, and what needs to change for you to move forward?

Ask yourself, and answer honestly, what do you want? What type of relationship do you want? What type of marriage do you want? Are you just staying in a relationship because it's convenient, or is your partner really the person you want to spend the rest of your life with? What do you want in your business? What type of role do you want? Only you know the answers to these questions, but unless you're truthful, you will keep their secrets hidden and will never be able to act on them. If you're not happy with your business, your body, your relationships, or your mindset the way they are, what are you doing or not doing that's causing this situation? Is there a relationship between your core values and your struggle to satisfy your vision for any of *The 4 Keys*?

Think ahead to your future self and what your life will be like if you applied the foundations starting today: *Do the work. No excuses. Always ready. Speak the truth.* If you lived your life by these, what could you achieve in just three months? In five years?

BREAKING NEGATIVE PATTERNS

Living by the foundations gives you the power to break the negative patterns that restrict you and impact those around you. You'll be able to develop new habits and behaviours that serve you much better.

My dad was a great cricketer at one point in his life. If he'd wanted to, he could have at least played at county level. One day, when I was about ten, I said to him, 'Dad, I really love cricket. There's a local club I'd like to join. I think I'm pretty good at this.' He turned to me and said, 'Yeah, you'll never play cricket.' This stung, more so because it was so out of character for my usually optimistic and supportive father. Years later, after my dad died, I was watching pro ice hockey on TV with my granddad. I said, 'I'm going to play in that league one day.' He turned to me and said, 'You'll never play in that league.' It was like a lightbulb went on. I asked Granddad about Dad's cricket, and he was dismissive and negative, focusing on the times my dad misbehaved or didn't show up.

All those years ago, my dad had simply been repeating a pattern. He was projecting onto me the very same experience he'd had with his own dad. To break away from that negative cycle, I've always made a conscious effort to be positive and supportive with my children because I don't want to recreate that pattern and project my negative experience onto them. This is a prime example of letting go of things that don't serve us and also of how we can use negative experiences to shape ourselves in a positive way. There are still times when I try to justify my behaviour because I think my dad would respect it or encourage it. Then I realise that if I'm having to justify it to myself, that doesn't sit comfortably with me and doesn't fit with my values.

When you're starting to make changes, there's a tension between your ingrained, hardwired behaviours based on instinct and experience, which take over when you're in the moment, and the pre-frontal cortex that engages with values and thought-based decision-making. But as you get used to making choices based on your new-found values, those values become more habitual and instinctive, so they will become your go-to, in-the-moment behaviours. The brain is plastic and malleable, and it's this neuroplasticity that allows us to make these changes.

Run-of-the-mill coaching, whether it's in sports, business, or life-coaching, can get a little bit stale and wishy-washy. It's often all style and no substance, just empty words that sound great but don't instil action and real change. My philosophy is that we're all here, all experiencing life, so let's be honest. Let's speak the truth about how we feel and behave. Find out what's working and what isn't. Identify the change we want to make.

On a deeper level, living with proper values that drive you isn't so much about what you do or say, but more about how you make other people feel. I don't remember a lot of details about that conversation with my dad about me playing cricket. What really stands out for me is how he made me feel. He made me feel like I just wasn't good enough. If my dad were still alive, I doubt he'd even remember that conversation because, as adults, we often don't think about what we say. A flippant comment like that stays with a child and can have a huge impact as they mature.

Has there been a time in your life when you experienced a similar event? Do you think it's affected the way you behave or the core values you adopted? Would you like to redefine those values to better suit your vision? You can do this. You are not wedded to old values that hold you back.

Adopting the foundations will make the people around you feel better because they will know they can trust you. Think about it: if you always do the work, make no excuses, are always ready and completely honest about how you feel and what you want in life, the people around you will come to know you as a person they can rely on who won't mislead them or put them in uncomfortable or precarious situations. This goes both ways: if the people around you also live by these values, you will feel better because you'll be able to trust them and be better prepared to predict your day-to-day outcomes with them – no unwelcome surprises. Those feelings are what hardwire the brain and shape who you are, especially as a growing child; but you can change your brain, remember? And if your way of thinking is holding you back, you need to change your way of thinking. The first step is to make those changes, step by step, and see how this changes your behaviour, how it changes the way people respond to you, and ultimately, how it assists you in advancing towards your vision in each of *The 4 Keys*.

These are the Get Fit To Win Foundations – do the work, no excuses, always ready, and speak the truth – that work well for me and others in my Get Fit To Win Mastermind group. They fit my vision and my aspirations across *The 4 Keys*. You can use these because they'll give you a great foundation, or you can come up with your own if these don't quite fit with your own visions. Core values will also help you get the most from the 90-Day Reset.

One last point I would like to make here is that I don't hold a grudge against my parents for anything they did to shape me during my upbringing, especially anything that didn't serve me as a child or later as an adult. Being a parent is hard, and I believe most parents want their children to be happy. My mum gave me the power to be a free thinker, which has had an incredibly positive impact on my life. She has been completely non-judgemental and allowed me the freedom to learn from my own mistakes. She very rarely held me accountable, and whilst this instilled some poor behaviours, I wouldn't change it all. I also see the positive impact she has on my eldest daughter, Izzie, who is 19. My mother is the strongest person I know, and she continues to empower me. She survived all the tough times of my early years, lost her husband, my dad, and she lost an eye to cancer. We love each other unconditionally, and that absolute love *is* a pattern I chose to repeat with my own children. Empowerment and free thinking are also essential qualities in business leaders.

Not only must you be strong and mentally agile, but to be truly successful and build the strongest teams, you must be able to empower those around you, encouraging rather than stifling ideas, independent thought, and creativity.

LIVE YOUR VALUES

Living your values across *The 4 Keys* takes practice, and it can be helpful to have a daily reminder to keep yourself on the right path. You may be better at doing the work or not making excuses in one or two keys but be struggling with these values across the others, and that's where reminders and prompts can be particularly useful. Daily reminders stop you from falling back into old patterns and habits that don't bring you closer to your vision.

Having prompts on fridge magnets, mouse mats, T-shirts, and posters is great, and these act as useful visual reminders, but it has to go deeper than that. Following these core values is more than merely reading the words. Read them and then execute them – live them. Behave as you want others to behave. Set exemplary standards based on your values and inspire others to follow suit. If I want my kids to do the work and be conscientious, honest, and reliable, I have to be that way too. If I want the groups I work with to do the work, then so do I. If you want your kids to eat healthily, be kind in their relationships, conscientious in their work, and resilient, then you have to do it consistently in front of them. I'm constantly striving to be a role model to those around me. I firmly believe in the truth of Gandhi's famous quote, 'Be the change you wish to see in the world.' Live your values, because when you do, you'll start to experience real, meaningful results. You will have real 'aha moments' when your actions promote outcomes that are aligned with your vision.

EXERCISE: YOUR VALUES IN ACTION

What patterns and values have *you* identified for yourself? Are they the same as the Get Fit To Win Foundations, or do you have different ones? Which ones serve you? Which ones do you need to break or replace? Jot them down in two lists: values you want to practise and those you wish to change.

Now take action. Right now. Don't procrastinate. Just do the work. Make a start. If one of your values is, like mine, 'do the work', and you're thinking about launching that blog or calling a potential client to close a deal, do it now. Take action. Put yourself out there.

1. Do The Work.
    ◦ Do you find yourself procrastinating, overthinking, and avoiding taking action?

2. No Excuses.

- Does your inner voice and way of thinking hold you back?

3. Speak the Truth.
   - Are you being true to yourself about what you want in your life?

4. Always Ready.
   - Do you make wrong choices today that will stop you from achieving your vision?

Your values should enable you to lead the life you should be living.

PART II

TURN YOUR VISION INTO REALITY

CHAPTER 5

GET RESULTS FOCUSED

Your time is limited, so don't waste it living someone else's life. Don't be trapped by dogma – which is living with the results of other people's thinking. Don't let the noise of others' opinions drown out your own inner voice. And most important, have the courage to follow your heart and intuition.

—STEVE JOBS

It's time to get outside your comfort zone and start making real changes. In Part 2, you'll be focusing on your 90-Day Reset, which hundreds of business leaders in the Get Fit To Win community have used to accelerate their results and achieve their vision faster. You'll need your journal handy for this section!

THE 90-DAY RESET

Your vision might seem a little broad or even fantastical right now, but you'll segment it into tangible goals and results across all four keys that you'll execute over the next 90 days.

Whether you've got a three-year, 12-month or 20-year vision, you'll make great strides within the 90-day game plan. You'll reflect on the type of person you are: whether you're someone who is naturally results-driven and tends to jump straight to trying to drive up the bottom line, or someone who is more reflective but who perhaps isn't always good at getting clear on what needs to be done. You'll focus on getting results in 90 days but see results at your 30- and 60-day benchmarks. You'll review your progress weekly during the course of the game plan, to establish what's working and what needs more work. You'll assess whether you're heading in the right direction, staying agile, needing to make some changes, or trying different tactics.

To achieve this, we'll explore the following questions in each key:

1. What is the single biggest challenge you are facing in your business, body, relationships, and mindset?
2. What are your desired outcomes for each key in 90 days?

3. What options and ideas do you have that will help you achieve your desired outcome?
4. How will you turn your ideas into a specific, measurable, attainable, relevant and timely (SMART) targets?

STRETCH YOUR GOALS

Whether you're a sports team or a business, the principles for going beyond your comfort zone are the same. In the film *Facing Giants*, there's a scene I share in the Get Fit To Win workshop. It's a little cheesy, although for some, it is very emotive and inspiring. The coach is communicating with his players, and one guy, Brock, has this limiting belief. He doesn't think they can win their next game.

The coach turns to him and says, 'Have you written Friday night off as a loss, Brock, already? Have you written the game off?'

Brock responds, 'Not if I think we can beat them.'

The coach takes the team outside and runs a drill called the Death Crawl. Brock has to carry one of his teammates on his back, crawling with just hands and feet. The coach asks Brock how far he thinks he can get, and Brock says, 'I think I can get to thirty yards with Jeremy on my back.'

The coach says, 'No. I think you can get to fifty yards with

Jeremy on your back. I'm going to blindfold you because I don't want you quitting when you think you've gone far enough.'

They proceed, with Brock carrying Jeremy, and he gets to a point where he's in a lot of pain.

The rest of the team start laughing, saying, 'He's never going to get to fifty.'

The coach shouts encouragement, saying, 'twenty more yards, five more yards', and so on.

When Brock takes off his blindfold, he sees that he's actually gone *100 yards*. For Brock, his comfort zone was 30 yards, and his stretch was 50. He was limiting himself with his belief. Once his limits were removed, he had the capacity to attain 100 yards.

I experienced this first-hand as head coach of Team GB Inline Hockey. We were the lowest seed, and the Czechs were the highest, yet I believed we could steal points in the Pool A group against Team Czech and Team Finland. It wasn't just delusion; I knew with the right tactics we could upset them. But tactics are useless without belief. We had to believe in our tactics, and we had to believe we could win. I remember texting the captain my thoughts. I texted, 'We have an opportunity to beat the Czechs, who are the highest seed as world championships.' He thought I had been drinking! In the end, we tied the Czechs and beat the Finns.

PLAYING SAFE IS RISKY

I've missed over 9,000 shots in my career.
I've lost almost 300 games.
Twenty-six times I've been trusted to take the game-winning shot and missed.
I've failed over and over and over again in my life.
And that is why I succeed.

—MICHAEL JORDAN

As a business leader, you may need to take risks during your 90-Day Reset and embrace the unknown to achieve your vision.

On Team GB, one of our mantras was 'Playing safe is risky'. Whilst there are times when it is appropriate to play safe, it is also a sign of complacency or avoiding a perceived threat. You'll see players turn away from their opponent, failing to execute a play in the hope they won't make a mistake or get turned over. It is a sign of nerves, the inner voice keeping them safe when really, they need to be on the offence. This is as true in business as it is in sports. Playing it safe can prevent you from moving forward and reaching your full potential, but you can commit to being on the offence and going for the win.

Executing your 90-Day Reset will require the right mindset to deal with your inner voice that will try to derail you. The reset is about going all in, so timing is key. It's about action that keeps you motivated and driven; you'll need to keep your purpose at the forefront of your mind as a daily reminder of your why. This keeps you going forward and frees you of any fear and anxiety about the outcomes attached to risk that keep you in your comfort zone. If you play it safe, you'll never reach your full potential. Commit, be on the offence, and go for the win!

CHOOSE IMPORTANCE OVER URGENCY

At first glance, it may seem that all your goals are important, and they probably are. However, some are urgent while others are non-urgent. Focus on your non-urgent goals in the 90-day game plan – things you don't have to do and would normally put off forever. These are the goals that constantly take a back seat to your urgent goals but have the greatest impact on your life. The only caveat here is that if you are in danger of having a heart attack or losing an important relationship, or if your business is in danger of going under because you have neglected critical behaviours or activities, correcting those issues are urgent *and* important. I truly hope you are not in any

KNOW YOUR TENDENCIES

People have different tendencies in the way they approach their objectives in the 90-Day Reset, and that's perfectly acceptable. There is not one way to do the reset. Maybe you recognise yourself in one of these descriptions?

Results-Driven Leader: When developing your 90-Day game plan, you will be mostly focused on output and delivering results. This is absolutely key for achieving your vision. You must also be mindful that you can become frustrated when results are not happening fast enough. This can impact others and cause stress for both you and those around you. Be patient with yourself and others rather than demanding results. Your attempt to control may end in loss of control. Your motto is 'Get it done and don't waste time.'

Process-Driven Leader: When creating your 90-day game plan, you will want to create efficient processes and systems that will ensure certainty and clarity. You will like to have measures in place so that you can check the quality of your work. These are essential to increasing a consistent performance; however, you will need to be mindful that it will feel restrictive for those around you who may not meet your standards. Whilst planning is important, you will need to embrace change and be flexible with your game plan. Your motto is, 'I can't move on until I get it right.'

Consensus-Driven Leader: When developing your 90-day game plan, you will want to ensure it is in harmony with your personal relationships. Values are important to you, as you want balance and a calm environment. Creating the right culture is essential to high performance; however, you will also need to keep the end in mind and not lose sight of the goal. Whilst reflection is a good thing, delivery of results and action will make your vision happen. Your motto tends to be: 'Don't rock the boat.'

Image-Driven Leader: When developing your 90-day game plan, you will have a preference towards external perception, personal image, and how you show up. It is important that you of those situations, but if you are, they obviously require your immediate attention. In the case of my marriage, I needed to act fast. I'd allowed things to become urgent by neglecting the non-urgent things in my relationship. For the most part, though, your goals in the 90-day game plan will address outcomes that bring you closer to your vision but that you have been neglecting for some time because you have not seen them as urgent or because no one has been holding you accountable. This is where you have to hold yourself accountable and become your own best friend.

To visualise your most important goals, imagine a big jar, some large rocks, small stones, sand, and water. To get everything in the jar, you need to put the rocks in first. Which of your goals are the rocks? What is that one thing in your business that you procrastinate over or that you talk with your colleagues about most but never take action on? What's that one thing in your relationship? Concerning your physical fitness? Your mindset? These are your rocks.

You can't tackle every one of your goals simultaneously, because even though you're going all in on your 90-day game plan, life and business go on. You can't ignore them either, because you're working towards improving them. Take aggressive action in manageable chunks. Choose four targets that are really going to bring value to your life and others. One can be as simple as getting that website up that you've been talking about for a year or launching a YouTube channel. Another can be having a weekly date night with your spouse, playing football or another sport every Friday evening with your kids, or going for a hike with the whole family every weekend.

Go fast, learn quick. Be aggressive in your actions. Build time in weekly to take action towards your vision. Engage in agile thinking and embrace failure. You may not win every time, but if you can learn from it, soon you'll be winning consistently every day. Win the days, and the years will take care of themselves. As Buddhist monk Thích Nhất Hạnh says, 'The best way to take care of the future is to take care of the present moment.' Each week, set aside 30 minutes to review your progress and learn from your decisions.

Ask yourself what is working well for me, what are my successes? What could I be doing differently to improve? What one action can I take into next week that will move me forward in *The 4 Keys*?

YOUR 90-DAY RESET

How are you going to complete your 90-day game plan? Are you going to stay entrenched in your comfort zone, or are you going to stretch? Remember, your comfort zone, just like your brain, is elastic and malleable. Think of a rubber band. Stretch that band out and keep it there for 90 days. When you let it go, it's bigger than it was before. The same applies to your comfort zone. You'll stretch yourself for 90 days, then you can go back to your comfort zone, but your comfort zone will be bigger than before. If you commit to stretching yourself for 90 days, you'll develop new neural pathways in the brain, learn things about yourself and maybe even exceed your own expectations, and you'll reap the benefits. The 90-Day Reset will move your business forward. You'll be fitter, stronger, and ready for whatever comes your way, and most importantly, your personal relationships will be thriving.

Look at your visions across *The 4 Keys* and ask yourself if they stretch you. Maybe your business vision is to turn over £5 million this year. You know you'll achieve it because you did it last year, so that's not much of a stretch. How about stretching that vision to £7 million or shifting your focus to increasing profit? What would you have to do to make that a reality? What would need to change? Whether your goal is £100K or £100 million, don't worry about *how* yet. We'll get to that. Your 90-Day Reset will get you there.

Perhaps you go to the gym every day, but you want to be more consistent or lift heavier, or maybe you want to enter a Tough Mudder? Maybe you already run half-marathons, in which case you could make your stretch goal to improve your time. Stop limiting yourself and see your potential instead of your limits. Right now, you might not believe that you can do it, but that doesn't matter because you *are* going to do it. You're going to put yourself out there and do something, even if it's not perfect. First, you'll put a plan together to make sure you're ready.

MASTERMIND EXAMPLE: 90-DAY RESET

Here's an example of a 90-Day Reset that came from Mark Baker, who is one of my Get Fit To Win Mastermind participants. You'll see there is a mix of metrics and plenty of non-urgent, big-picture objectives.

1. Business Key:
   - Improve profit per salesperson and increase overall business profitability by 12 per cent
   - Change commission plan to reward overachievers and pay less for those under target

2. Body Key:
   - Lose a stone (6.5KG)

- ○ Do 3–4 gym sessions a week and 1 × 15-minute HIIT session at home per week
- ○ Stick to a healthier diet and no alcohol at home during the week

3. Relationship Key:
   - ○ Arrange a date night every week
   - ○ Spend more quality time with my daughters (even though they're grown up, independent, and busy doing their own thing – I don't see them enough)

4. Mindset Key:
   - ○ A minimum of ten minutes of meditation per day
   - ○ Take time out for a 15 to 20-minute walk at lunch-time to get out the office and away from the desk every day

STEP-BY-STEP 90-DAY RESET

Begin your own 90-Day Reset with the following steps. You don't have to do them all at once, but try to make some progress on the first step right now.

THE 4 KEYS 90-DAY RESET MATRIX

Start by drawing the matrix in your journal per the example shown below to represent each key in *The 4 Keys* programme. Your matrix incorporates your single biggest challenges, your desired outcomes, your options, and SMART – specific, measurable, attainable, relevant, and time frame – objectives in each key.

4 KEYS 90-DAY RESET MATRIX

BUSINESS	
Your Single Biggest Challenge	
Your Desired 90-Day Outcome	
Options and Ideas	
S.M.A.R.T. Targets	
BODY	
Your Single Biggest Challenge	
Your Desired 90-Day Outcome	
Options and Ideas	
S.M.A.R.T. Targets	
RELATIONSHIPS	
Your Single Biggest Challenge	
Your Desired 90-Day Outcome	
Options and Ideas	
S.M.A.R.T. Targets	
MINDSET	
Your Single Biggest Challenge	
Your Desired 90-Day Outcome	
Options and Ideas	
S.M.A.R.T. Targets	

STEP 1: WHAT IS THE SINGLE BIGGEST CHALLENGE YOU ARE FACING RIGHT NOW?

It's likely that you have many challenges, but I'm asking you to focus on one per key. This may be difficult for you to decide, but I encourage you to choose the one challenge you believe will have the biggest impact within each key in the next 90 days.

If you're like most entrepreneurs and business leaders, there are many things that keep you up at night. This is often referred to as the '3 a.m. club'. They lie wide awake, wondering how the hell they're going to fix some of the challenges they face...sound familiar?

It's no wonder we don't have the headspace for the other facets of our lives when running a business. I sometimes think it would be much easier to get a nine-to-five job with a boss telling me what to do and avoid the stress of leading a team or running a business. But, like you, I appreciate the upside of working with my team and running my own business.

You won't be able to fix *everything* in your life and business, but you'll be able to focus on the other problems you're facing in your *next* 90-Day Reset. One reset at a time, and you'll experience dramatic progress. Take on too much at once, and you could be overwhelmed.

I started my first coaching business at 22. It was called Let's Get Rolling. I specialised in roller-hockey tuition, and I organised hockey schools throughout the UK. I loved it. The problem was scaling the business. All the work was on weekends, apart from school holidays. The business was built around my name, and the clubs and players wanted me to run the camps. It was impossible to scale. I would lie awake at night thinking about creating a tutorial video which would help me reach more people and scale the business, but I never did. It was an idea that never turned into action. Like many entrepreneurs, I was focused on urgent matters and letting the opportunity to tackle non-urgent projects that could make a vast difference in my business slip away.

Fast-forward 20 years, and I found that I had the exact same problem with Get Fit To Win. I realised I would never achieve my purpose of enabling one million business owners to live the lives they want if I couldn't scale the business. This had other implications, such as time away from home and staying healthy on the road. It wasn't until I focused on my non-urgent objectives that I was able to create tutorial videos for *The 4 Keys* and write this book.

Take a moment to think about your single biggest challenge in each key. Here were mine from September 2017:

4 KEYS 90-DAY RESET MATRIX

BUSINESS	
Your Single Biggest Challenge	*Scaling the Get Fit To Win business globally*
Your Desired 90-Day Outcome	
Options and Ideas	
S.M.A.R.T. Targets	

BODY	
Your Single Biggest Challenge	*Chronic arthritis*
Your Desired 90-Day Outcome	
Options and Ideas	
S.M.A.R.T. Targets	

RELATIONSHIPS	
Your Single Biggest Challenge	*Quality time with my family*
Your Desired 90-Day Outcome	
Options and Ideas	
S.M.A.R.T. Targets	

MINDSET	
Your Single Biggest Challenge	*Feeling too stretched mentally and emotionally*
Your Desired 90-Day Outcome	
Options and Ideas	
S.M.A.R.T. Targets	

STEP 2: WHAT IS YOUR DESIRED OUTCOME IN 90 DAYS?

In this step, you will start to think about your desired outcome. It doesn't need to be metric-focused at this stage; it is about what you want to improve in your business and life. You may focus on how you want to feel or make others feel.

Here are my 90-day desired outcomes aligned to my single biggest challenges:

4 KEYS 90-DAY RESET MATRIX

BUSINESS

Your Single Biggest Challenge	*Scaling the Get Fit To Win business globally*
Your Desired 90-Day Outcome	*Create a business model that will reach more people beyond what I can achieve face-to-face*
Options and Ideas	
S.M.A.R.T. Targets	

BODY

Your Single Biggest Challenge	*Chronic arthritis*
Your Desired 90-Day Outcome	*To be pain-free and avoid inflammatory attacks*
Options and Ideas	
S.M.A.R.T. Targets	

RELATIONSHIPS

Your Single Biggest Challenge	*Quality time with my family*
Your Desired 90-Day Outcome	*Ensure my wife feels confident I am there for her when she needs me most and can support her better with the children*
Options and Ideas	
S.M.A.R.T. Targets	

MINDSET

Your Single Biggest Challenge	*Feeling too stretched mentally and emotionally*
Your Desired 90-Day Outcome	*Create more headspace and time to slow down to reflect on my 4 keys*
Options and Ideas	
S.M.A.R.T. Targets	

STEP 3: WHAT ARE YOUR OPTIONS AND IDEAS?

What options and ideas do you have that will help you achieve your desired outcome?

This is where you get creative by giving yourself five minutes to come up with as many ideas as you can to achieve your desired outcome. This time limit keeps you from

4 KEYS 90-DAY RESET MATRIX

BUSINESS	
Your Single Biggest Challenge	Scaling the Get Fit To Win business globally
Your Desired 90-Day Outcome	Create a business model that will reach more people beyond what I can achieve face-to-face
Options and Ideas	• Build a bigger team of Get Fit To Win Coaches • Create online programme • Create an online mastermind group • Write a book
S.M.A.R.T. Targets	

BODY	
Your Single Biggest Challenge	Chronic arthritis
Your Desired 90-Day Outcome	To be pain-free and avoid inflammatory attacks
Options and Ideas	• Vegan diet • Paleo diet • Mediterranean diet • Ketogenic diet • Less intensive training
S.M.A.R.T. Targets	

RELATIONSHIPS	
Your Single Biggest Challenge	Quality time with my family
Your Desired 90-Day Outcome	Ensure my wife feels confident I am there for her when she needs me most and can support her better with the children
Options and Ideas	• Date nights • Weekly day trip • Take the kids away once a week to give my wife a break
S.M.A.R.T. Targets	

MINDSET	
Your Single Biggest Challenge	Feeling too stretched mentally and emotionally
Your Desired 90-Day Outcome	Create more headspace and time to slow down to reflect on my 4 keys
Options and Ideas	• Practice meditation • Practice box breathing • Complete a mindfulness course
S.M.A.R.T. Targets	

overthinking and motivates you to think and write. This is a brainstorming session, and there are no bad ideas at this point, so don't second-guess or judge yourself. At this stage, you are not committing to anything. Capture the ideas you think will help you achieve your desired outcome in your journal.

Then, follow up on some of your ideas. Do some online research, get some feedback from friends and colleagues, or speak with someone you know who has already achieved similar goals. As you get more information, start to fill in your matrix as shown.

STEP 4: TURN YOUR IDEAS INTO SMART TARGETS

By now, you have identified your single biggest challenge in each of your four keys, and you have also identified your desired outcomes and brainstormed ideas for each one. Now it's time to commit and go all in. You may find this part easy, or you may have found the process frustrating. Well done for being patient with the steps! Or you may find this part difficult, as now it is time to get results-focused so you can pull the trigger and make your desired outcomes a reality. You may also be thinking, *I can't choose one idea. I need to do them all.* This is where you get disciplined and choose the option that will move you forward the most in 90 days. Remember, you will be able to focus on others in your next 90-Day Reset. Be patient with yourself. If you think you have the capacity to take on more SMART targets in each key, then go for it.

You need to decide on the best ideas and turn them into SMART targets, making each one specific, measurable, attainable, and relevant, and giving each target a time frame. Once you've got all those ideas, take a step back and review them. Identify which one, in each key, you want to commit to for the next 90 days. Then make it a SMART goal:

- Specific. This involves establishing how you'll accomplish your desired outcome. What steps will you take? What will you focus on? What are your deliverables? *Don't be vague.*
- Measurable. How is the target measurable? How will you know if you're winning? Can you measure and track your success?
- Attainable. Is your goal attainable? Do you have the resources? The capacity? The skills? If you haven't got the resources, where will you find them? It is about making it happen, not making excuses. Time is also a factor here, but I'm going to arm you with some brilliant productivity tips, so you'll be able to find the time to achieve your desired outcome.
- Relevant. Are your specific targets and choices relevant to your vision and purpose? Do they fit with your why? Will it get you closer to that vision in 90 days?
- Time frame. What will you achieve in 30 days and in 60 days so you know you are tracking to achieve your target in 90 days?

Start now by jotting down your SMART targets.

MY SMART TARGETS
4 KEYS 90-DAY RESET MATRIX

BUSINESS

Your Single Biggest Challenge	Scaling the Get Fit To Win business globally
Your Desired 90-Day Outcome	Create a business model that will reach more people beyond what I can achieve face-to-face
Options and Ideas	• Build a bigger team of Get Fit To Win Coaches • Create online programme • Create an online mastermind group • Write a book
S.M.A.R.T. Targets	• Create an online mastermind group • With a minimum of 25 people • Share 3 updates/blogs per week • Launch by January 1, 2018 • Ensure all group members create their own 90-Day Resets

BODY

Your Single Biggest Challenge	Chronic arthritis
Your Desired 90-Day Outcome	To be pain-free and avoid inflammatory attacks
Options and Ideas	• Vegan diet • Paleo diet • Mediterranean diet • Ketogenic diet • Less intensive training
S.M.A.R.T. Targets	• Follow a Ketogenic/paleo eating plan • Measure number of inflammatory attacks • Shop weekly and prepare meals • Consistently follow a Paleo plan from January 1st - April 1st

RELATIONSHIPS

Your Single Biggest Challenge	Quality time with my family
Your Desired 90-Day Outcome	Ensure my wife feels confident I am there for her when she needs me most and can support her better with the children
Options and Ideas	• Date nights • Weekly day trip • Take the kids away once a week to give my wife a break
S.M.A.R.T. Targets	• Take the kids away once a week for a full day to give my wife a break • Give my wife time and space to start her own business • Every Saturday from January 1, 2018

MINDSET

Your Single Biggest Challenge	Feeling too stretched mentally and emotionally
Your Desired 90-Day Outcome	Create more headspace and time to slow down to reflect on my 4 keys
Options and Ideas	• Practice meditation • Practice box breathing • Complete a mindfulness course
S.M.A.R.T. Targets	• Get regular, honest feedback from the mastermind group • Measure level of engagement in the group and make changes based on feedback • Invest 30 minutes everyday to focus on Get Fit To Win business • Get weekly feedback from the mastermind group from January 1st

If you need some ideas, review these real-life, 90-Day Reset examples – which became success stories – from business owners who participated in my Get Fit To Win Mastermind:

EXAMPLE #1

1. Business Key
   - Three consistently profitable months of 30k+
   - Ensure all sales people are truly profitable by end of quarter
   - Get our USA team to break-even point

2. Body Key
   - Get down to 110 kg
   - Exercise daily
   - No alcohol at home for 90 days

3. Relationship Key
   - Date nights weekly (12 in 90 days)
   - Help wife get back to work within 90 days

4. Mindset Key
   - Use Headspace app daily
   - Continue monthly hypnocoaching sessions

EXAMPLE #2

1. Business Key
   - Achieve 90 plan set at the end of 2017
   - Hit financial targets
   - Reduce costs by 5%

2. Body Key
   - Drop eight pounds, then maintain weight and tone up
   - Three bootcamp HIIT sessions per week
   - Maintain healthy eating
   - Drinking alcohol only once per week maximum

3. Relationship Key
   - One date lunch per week with wife
   - One evening per week with teenage sons – if they let me!

4. Mindset Key
   - Time management course
   - Ten minutes of meditation per day in morning

EXAMPLE #3

1. Business Key
   - Create marketing strategy
   - Launch new brand
   - Launch new website

2. Body Key
   - In bed by 11 p.m. every night
   - Do posture stretches every morning
   - 2 × PT sessions a week, 1 × bike ride (with son) and 1 × golf round (also bonus goal is to win a competition at my new club)
   - And a plant-based smoothie to go with my Weetabix every morning

3. Relationship Key
   - One date a fortnight with my wife
   - Locking my phone away after 7.30 p.m. every night

4. Mindset key
   - Do five minutes on the Calm app every morning
   - Have a massage once a week to reset myself

Wish me luck!

Steve

You'll notice that some of the 90-Day Reset targets are SMARTer than others. It is up to you, although I encourage you to make them as tight as possible. In the Get Fit To Win Mastermind, people have found that the SMARTer their targets, the more successful they are in achieving them.

The one thing all the above have in common is all the targets are non-urgent, and they can get bumped. But what becomes urgent if we don't focus on the above?

WRITE DOWN YOUR FOUR KEY SMART TARGETS IN YOUR JOURNAL

Find a quiet place to think about your desired outcomes, your vision, and your purpose. Imagine yourself in 90 days, when your targets have become a reality. Be completely focused on what you want for yourself. My Get Fit To Win Mastermind group and many studies show that people are more likely to achieve their goals when they are held accountable. Why not share your SMART targets with friends or a coach? I don't necessarily recommend sharing your plan with those who are linked to your targets, such as your spouse. Instead, let your actions do the talking.

For example, here are mine from December 2017:

For my business key, I will create an online mastermind group with a minimum of 20 members within 30 days. I am aiming to share a minimum of three topics per week to ensure the group stays engaged and is well supported. I will hold all group members accountable to create their own 90-Day Resets. I will launch the mastermind by 1 January 2018. I will create a pilot series of videos to support the group and upload them to an online platform by 1 January 2018. I will also aim to post daily on LinkedIn about leadership challenges.

For my body key, I am going to give my body a rest from lifting weights and do body weight training four days per week to include pull-ups, burpees, press-ups, and squats. To manage my inflammation, I am going to follow a Paleo eating plan and remove sugar and grains (including beer) from my diet for 90 days. I will monitor the number of inflammatory attacks as a measure of success (hopefully zero). I will shop weekly and prepare meals for lunch. I will be consistent for 90 days.

For my relationship key, I want to help my wife start her own business. I will have our children one to two full days per week to give my wife a break and focus on coursework. The aim is to enable my wife to start her business by 1 April 2018. I also hope this gives us additional time and space to rebuild our own relationship.

For the mindset key, I want to remove any self-doubt about The 4 Keys *programme. To ensure the business and brand are on point, I will seek regular and brutally honest feedback from the mastermind group. I will start requesting weekly feedback from the mastermind group from 1 January 2018. I will present the concept to as many people as possible and start collecting feedback for a potential book.*

HAVE SMART 30-DAY AND 60-DAY BENCHMARKS

Depending on your targets, creating benchmarks could be as simple as dividing each one into three equal portions (and then aiming to reach each one every 30 days), but it could be more complex. If, for example, your 90-day goal is to make £100K but you start in January – which is a slow month, and February is only a little better – you're not going to do £33K each month. Perhaps you'll do £10K in January, £40K in February, and £50K in March. Just be mindful and realistic when establishing 30-day and 60-day benchmarks for your SMART objectives. This framework is pragmatic and takes all the emotion out of the equation, so if you're a results-driven person who tends to skip the preparation and dive right to the end, this process will slow you down and get you thinking more constructively. If you're a procrastinator or more reflective than reactive, this process will force you to start taking action in a well-paced, controlled way. Whatever your mindset, you'll be taking aggressive action for 90 days without burnout, and you'll experience the rewards of that action all year long.

This is not about working harder; it's about working smarter. Rather than working on these 90-day plans back-to-back all year, it's about compressing time and making the results of one 90-Day Reset last over the long term. During those 90 days when you go all in, you create an effect that's enduring and that you can sustain without much effort (remember, you've ventured beyond your comfort zone and 'stretched the rubber band') after the plan is over: getting long-term benefits from short-term action.

In the next chapter, we'll look at how to win daily to achieve your goals.

CHAPTER 6

WIN DAILY

If you take care of the minutes, the years will take care of themselves.

—TIBETAN PROVERB

By now, you've looked at the big picture. You've identified your vision and broken it down into SMART targets and 30-, 60-, and 90-day benchmarks, and you know where you're headed. It's time to start thinking about how to win the days. Remember, if you focus on the days, the years take care of themselves. To make daily progress, you will have to learn to be productive.

There are three types of people when it comes to productivity. The first group enjoys process and routine, and the more regimented the routine, the happier they are. These folks are naturally geared towards executing on their plan and meeting deadlines. The second group is those who are focused 'doers'. They have to consciously prepare themselves, structuring their daily plan to ensure they meet their goals. Routine doesn't come naturally to them; they have to work at it. This second group recognises that, even if they work well under pressure, the work they produce at the last minute isn't as good as it could have been. The third group are the last-minute heroes. These people genuinely believe that if they leave the work to the last minute, it'll get done. Last-minute heroes feel that this last-minute approach is perfectly acceptable, then they'll reflect on how they could've done better. They also put themselves under a lot of undue pressure that could have been avoided had they planned better. I used to be in the category but have learnt the hard way how to *not* be a last-minute doer!

DISCIPLINED PRODUCTIVITY

When I was growing up, there was very little routine or consistency in my home. Nobody ever sat me down and made me do my homework. I didn't have a regimented schedule at home, and I didn't apply myself at school. Even with hockey, I didn't think about preparing myself or planning my training, I just thought about playing hockey, getting fit, and getting strong. After I left school, I started my own business with a loan from the Princes Trust, for which I am forever grateful. It forced me to create a business plan and learn how to pitch, but I didn't have any processes in place, and I didn't get very far. Then I got my first 'real' job at a startup ski brand. This company didn't have any processes either. Everyone there, myself included, was winging it, from haphazard marketing to the way we'd receive and ship orders. In 2004, things weren't going well at the startup, and I told my boss that it wasn't working out. I had a good relationship with him, but he wasn't paying me on time. I told him I was going after another opportunity with Yellow Pages, and he replied, 'That's a tough gig. You're not going to get it.'

The recruitment process was extremely competitive, with 100 applicants for each open position. These roles were highly sought-after, with their good pay and great benefits. My recruitment agency managed to bypass most of the hiring rounds and got me straight in front of the interview panel. Two interviews later, I landed the job with Yellow Pages, and it changed my life. Their sales and management training was phenomenal, but the biggest lesson for me was productivity. Training lasted for three weeks, and keeping the job was even more challenging than getting it. After six months, of the six people who had joined my region, I was the only one left.

My brain is hardwired to thrive on and enjoy change and variety (and we'll talk more about this in Chapter 8, 'Embrace Change'), so processes and routines seemed exceptionally boring to me. However, once I got into it,

I appreciated the increased productivity and efficiency I got from systematising my work processes. It was as if something unlocked in me, a new organised version of me, which was a far cry from the version that thrived on chaos. It wasn't just about targets, it was about keeping on top of my work. I was given two sales campaigns a year, and I had to fill out my diary every day. I had to fill my schedule with between 16 and 20 meetings a week, so I'd set up four to five every day. I scheduled each day, with meetings spread throughout the morning and early afternoon, followed by time to do my artwork, get it reviewed, then pitch it two weeks later. I managed to organise the post codes so I could be more efficient with driving from client to client. This required being assertive with the client and totally in charge of my diary. By watching my colleagues, I learnt quickly who excelled and why. It all came down to productivity and organisation.

I had to own my diary. Completely. Whatever schedule I set for myself, it was imperative that I stuck to it, even if a client requested that I meet a little later or earlier. This was the biggest lesson I have kept with since my time at Yellow Pages – my diary. I am in charge of my diary, no excuses. I'm not going to compromise on my time. I recommend you have the same mindset when it comes to winning daily. It is the most precious thing in life.

For me to meet my targets there simply wasn't enough

time to accommodate changes and still get everything done, so I got into the habit of chunking my day and holding to the schedule. Even though this process didn't come naturally to me, it started to pay off immediately. This daily management is key to optimising your productivity and winning every day.

START HARD

In sports like hockey, coaches will tell you that the more aggressive you are in your opponent's end, the more time you have in your own. This principle holds true when scheduling your day for business, body, relationships, and mindset. Taking action at the beginning of the day or the week gives you momentum and potentially more time at the end of the day or week because you've already gotten the heavy lifting out the way.

Winning the game daily means you have to start your day off right, so a morning routine is essential. Morning chaos is a challenge many people face – especially parents – but setting a morning routine helps. Back in my days at Yellow Pages, I'd try to schedule my first meeting of the day for 8 a.m. I was a single parent during this period, so my early mornings were hectic. I'd get Izzie dressed, fed, drop her off at school or the grandparents, and drive to my first sales meeting. A routine makes you more productive and efficient and sets your day up the right way.

Remember that you won't win every day. If you do, your goals are probably too easy, and if they're hard and you still managed to hit them daily, you'd get complacent and start to slack off. Getting it right most of the time is perfectly okay. Don't beat yourself up on the tough days. Just take a breath and get straight back on the horse. Even if you fail two days in a row, you can get yourself back on track.

HIT EVERY KEY

Start each day by taking a decisive step towards meeting at least one of your four key goals. For your business goal, you can start your day by learning something new that's in line with your vision for your work. Listen to a podcast, read a post, write a blog, or create a video.

The way you schedule your day and attack productivity may be affected by the type of person you are. You may be process-driven, results-driven, consensus-driven, or image-driven, and the corresponding traits can help you in some cases and hold you back in others when it comes to managing your schedule for maximum productivity and goal management. Whether you're motivated by concern about how you appear to others or purely focused on achieving results, a procrastinator who spends too much time on process without taking any action or is so reflective that you're stuck in the moment or is mostly concerned with the impact you have on other people, your style may or may not serve you.

For your body key, get your heart rate up early in the day. Whether you're training for a triathlon and you need to practise high-intensity endurance training, you're brand new to trying to get in shape, or you're somewhere in the middle, find the training that works for you. It could be 20 minutes in the gym or on a run, or it could be a five- or ten-minute high-intensity interval training (HIIT) session. If you have a stationary bike, hop on for five or ten minutes and get your heart pounding before you jump in the shower. All the research shows that getting your heart rate up in the morning is good for your cognitive function and your mental health, as well as the physical benefits. Don't forget nutrition too. Make sure you eat a healthful breakfast to fuel your body properly for the day ahead. I recommend a protein-based breakfast over a high-carb breakfast, such as cereal. This will limit insulin production and keep you energised and satiated longer. I'm a strong advocate of following an intermittent fasting routine in which you eat during a compressed window – usually between four to eight hours each day. This has been shown to stimulate human growth hormone, cell repair, and gene expression, which provide protection against disease and are very important as we age. The combination of this type of fasting and a HIIT session has been shown to provide huge health benefits.

At Get Fit To Win, we take a primal approach to keeping fit and healthy, inspired by Mark Sissons, author of *The Primal Blueprint*,[7] which I discuss in more detail in my Get Primal course. Always reflect your body's ability before doing any training.

- Strength training (weights or body weight) two times per week: hugely important to stave off the ageing process.
- Move slowly daily: walk, yoga, stretching at home. Take your time, stay present, and enjoy the environment you are in.
- Sprint: there is no better way to get strong and lean. Try 8 × 8–15 second sprints once per week. It's all you need to do and will take 15–20 minutes, which includes a warm-up and cool-down. You can also sprint on a bike or rowing machine, or swim if running doesn't work for you due to injury.
- Be playful: enjoy a hobby, climb a tree, mess around with the kids, play tag, go roller blading. It's about getting back to your child state and having some fun!

You can hit the relationship key by being present with your partner and children. Be thankful and loving towards them and let them know how much you value them. Pitch in and do your fair share regarding housework and

---

7   Mark Sisson, *The Primal Blueprint: Reprogram Your Genes for Effortless Weight Loss, Vibrant Health, and Boundless Energy* (Malibu: Primal Nutrition, 2012).

parenting. Send your loved one an early morning text or leave a note to let them know you're thinking of them.

For your mindset key, get into your calm, pregame state. Spend five minutes or longer deep-breathing or try a five-minute meditation – whatever works for you. Be aware of what causes you stress too. If a certain part of your commute causes a lot of frustration, see if there's another route you can take. It may take longer to get to the office, but leaving a few minutes earlier each day may be worth it if you arrive in a calmer state of mind. Get calm, clear, focused, and mentally prepared to face your daily challenges.

This is your framework, so experiment and create a routine that works for you. We're all different, so develop a routine you can stick to that fits your lifestyle. Once this routine becomes habit, you'll do it automatically. Try it for 21 days and you'll see it gets easier as it becomes habitual, and you'll also start seeing the benefits. If you hold on to the idea of hitting your four keys daily, you will move forward. If you take care of the days, the years will take care of themselves.

PRODUCTIVITY PERIODS

Chunking your day into 'periods' helps you stay organised, makes it easier to stay on task with your objectives, and increases your productivity. I split my day into four periods.

PERIOD 1

Period 1 is pre-8 a.m. During this time, hit at least one of *The 4 Keys* before you leave the house and then follow through with the rest of your morning routine. When I was the most productive, I was hitting all four keys in Period 1, but start with one and then work your way to adding more if you have the time. I would aim to write my LinkedIn blog post before 8 a.m.

PERIOD 2

Period 2 is 8 a.m. to 10 a.m. This and Period 3 comprise the prenoon chunks when you should focus on non-urgent tasks. Urgent tasks will obviously crop up or require you to attend to them right away, but always plan to be tackling two to three important, but not urgent, tasks. Fire-fighting the urgent stuff doesn't tell us if we're winning or losing the day. It's the completion of the non-urgent tasks that indicates winning. Consider three non-urgent but import-ant things related to your business – those bigger things that you never seem to get around to doing, like writing a book, launching a blog, starting a YouTube channel, or redesigning your website. Break them down and figure out what you need to do to make them happen. If you want to write a book, for example, set aside time in one of your morning periods to write 500 words. It's about taking focused action. If you want to close X amount of deals before the end of the week/month/year, what smaller steps do you need to take to get there? Sure, you could put this non-urgent stuff off, but remember, we're on the offence, taking aggressive action, making time at the end of the day or week to deal with urgent stuff, or to enjoy more free time. It's delayed gratification.

PERIOD 3

Period 3 is 10 a.m. to 12 p.m. and, like Period 2, is reserved for important but non-urgent activities. This is where the hard work is.

Imagine your day as a cherry-iced bun. Let's say the nicest bits are the cherry and the icing, so start with the dry bun. Once you've eaten that, move on to the icing and finish with the cherry. This equates to delayed, but more pleasurable, gratification. Doing your non-urgent but very important tasks before noon delivers the best results, because after noon, your cognitive ability starts to wane. You become more fatigued, so you're not performing at your best.

If you find, particularly in the early days of turning this routine into a habit, that you're struggling to stick with it consistently, remind yourself of why you're doing this. Re-examine your why, look at the long-term gains and the benefits you're seeing already. Try putting a picture of something that reminds you of your why on your desk or the screensaver on your phone. It keeps the why alive and fresh in your mind so it doesn't get buried by all the fire-fighting and daily monotony.

What you achieve in Periods 2 and 3 won't necessarily make you instant money, but executing those tasks sets you up for long-term gains. For example, I posted daily on LinkedIn as part of one of my game-plan programmes, and from that, I secured over £80,000 of work in a short period, and, in fact, I'm still getting work off the back of those posts today. I didn't get paid to write them at the time, but the long-term gains have been immense.

The three daily tasks you choose to focus on in Periods 2 and 3 depend on your role and your long-term goals. As a business leader, you might want to focus on building the right team, or you may be more inclined to get out onto the pitch yourself to close deals – perhaps mentoring your people in the process. To get these activities right, know which 'hats' you're wearing: strategic, which focuses on high-level, long-term results for your business; operational, which concerns the overall management of the business; or tactical, the day-to-day activities that keep the business running. Imagine running a premiership football club...

PERIOD 4

Period 4 is noon onward. During this time, you need to identify what things you need to do, and by what time. Period 4 is reserved for urgent tasks that *have* to be completed. It's also for those things you really enjoy doing or get the biggest sense of achievement from. These are your cherries from the iced-bun analogy. Plus, if they are particularly urgent, your adrenaline will be pumping, and you'll be more likely to successfully execute them on time.

You have to get into that entrepreneurial mindset. Don't just assume that because you're a business leader, you can work whenever you want. That thinking kills your productivity, meaning you end up working really long days without accomplishing much and neglecting other facets of your life. If you want to be home to your family by 6 p.m., what tasks do you need to complete in Period 4, and what time do you need to leave the office? Plan it and stick to it.

BALANCE THE DAY-TO-DAY AND THE BIG PICTURE

What sort of process needs to be in place for you to achieve your targets? How can you measure your suc-

PRODUCTIVITY TIPS

Productivity apps are great. I used Minimalist for writing this book, following the Pomodoro method. Evernote, Asana, and Basecamp are useful project-management apps, particularly if you're working collaboratively. They help keep you and your team on task and your projects well organised. For personal productivity, there are a range of apps that can help, like those that let you chunk your time into 90-minute intervals, or the 25/5 Pomodoro method, which involves working for 25 minutes, then taking a five-minute break.

Plan each day the prior evening. Create your schedule for the following day and set aside some time before bed to review what tomorrow looks like.

Don't be beholden to your email. Work in 15-minute chunks, like at 9 a.m., 1 p.m., and 5 p.m., and only check and respond to emails during these times; otherwise, it can become a procrastination tool. If you interrupt your task every time you get a new email, you'll never be truly productive because, once interrupted, it can take 20 minutes or longer to refocus and pick up where you left off.

Take big tasks and break them into smaller ones. This ensures you aren't overwhelmed and helps you feel like you're making progress.

Celebrate the wins – not just your own but everyone's. If you have a team, celebrate their individual and collaborative wins. Nobody will celebrate your wins for you, particularly if you're a business leader, so take time out each day to celebrate all the little wins you've achieved that day. How you do this is up to you.

cess? What are the three important but non-urgent things you're going to tackle daily? How will you know if you're winning? How can you measure the quality of your work? If these questions are bouncing around in your head, don't worry. You're going to figure it all out.

As you begin to tackle each of your SMART objectives, you will need to find balance between being results-driven and knowing when to step back. Don't obsess over every little thing being perfect. That leads to procrastination and will prevent you from making real progress.

You have your SMART objectives prepared for each of *The 4 Keys*, and now you want to put them into the periods of your daily schedule. Sketch this out or put it in your daily planner or calendar – whatever you use to plan your day. If you don't have some type of daily planner, try a few different types and find one you like. I like wall planners so I can lay everything out visually, all in one place. With a large wall planner, you can see when you need to make calls, deadlines that are approaching, appointments, and so on. Other people like to use technology, like online calendars or apps to keep them on track, or a combination of physical and virtual aids. Experiment and see what works best for you.

While for some, this process may at first seem a little stifling, it's just a framework, and you do have freedom within it to adapt and get creative. This is often where the magic happens. I have observed this in sports teams, and it's often influenced by culture. If you look at a regimented, process-driven football team like Germany, they play their systems, they are brilliant, and they have been consistent world champions – well synchronised, well organised, and precise. But because of their structure, they may be easily disruptable. A team, such as Brazil or France, which also uses systems but is given enough freedom for a little flair – a little magic – can rapidly turn a team like Germany inside-out. Unlike France, Germany's regimented play style arguably doesn't allow any freedom to counteract the creative and inspired play of a skilled and creative opponent. I've observed these cultural differences in business and come to realise that the framework is important, but leaving yourself open to identify and take advantage of unexpected opportunities is also important.

The same thing applies with this framework and your business. Create a solid foundation that lets you implement the right systems that make you more productive and efficient, but allow yourself freedom within your framework to adapt and be agile and make decisions based on your gut instincts. This framework should allow you the flexibility to change things up whenever you need to.

MAKE IT HAPPEN

Losing is part of the process...

Roger Federer has won an average of 55 per cent of his career points.

Successful stock traders can make huge profits winning 30 per cent of their trades.

Tiger Woods' career-winning percentage was barely 25 per cent in his prime!

As I've mentioned before, a winning/growth mindset is linked to an entrepreneurial mindset. We can't keep winning. We have to reinvest in ourselves, our businesses, and our resources. Winning the long game requires continuous change, which may result in short-term losses.

What do you need to reinvest in or change to create a sustainable future?

What losses do you need to tolerate to win the long game?

You won't win every day. That's a given. The key is to win the important things.

Losing is part of the process...

Roger Federer wins an average of 55 per cent of his points.

Successful traders can make huge profits winning 30 per cent of their trades.

Tiger Woods' career-winning percentage is barley 25 per cent!

As an employee, these stats would get you fired in a nine-to-five job, but *as an entrepreneur, you may fail more than you win.*

Yes, you're in the game every day and you play to win, but remember that failing at some things is okay, as long as you win when it counts. If you don't win the day, don't be distraught or despondent, and definitely do not give up. Failing at something is acceptable; accepting you're a failure is not. Take a step back, take a deep breath, pause and reset, and be ready for tomorrow.

At this point, you're emotionally connected to your vision, and you've started thinking about how to get more results-focused. You're thinking about how you're going to win daily when you can, and always win when it counts. You have a morning routine, you've identified your top three important but non-urgent tasks, and you've scheduled time every day to focus on them. You understand that there will always be important, urgent stuff that crops up and that you have the flexibility within your structured framework to allow you to confidently spend time reacting to those things in need of immediate attention. In the next chapter, we'll look at how to stay on track and stay in the present, how to maintain clarity, and how to get back into action after a loss.

CHAPTER 7

—

MANAGE THE MIST

Life is 10 percent what happens to you and 90 percent how you respond to it.

—LOU HOLTZ

Much stress is created from the uncertainty around our rapidly changing, increasingly digital world, which can bombard you with its never-ending supply of distractions and information overload. I refer to this as 'the mist'. In this chapter, you'll learn how to slow down, detach from all the chaos, and maintain clarity in the face of today's tumultuous world.

The best leaders I have worked with have the ability to manage their thoughts, feelings, and emotions. Essentially, they are able to manage the mist when they are under pressure. Developing the ability to stay present will increase your awareness, clarity of judgment, and decision-making. It will also enhance your gravitas and define your level of mental toughness.

When I first started my career in performance improvement, the focus of my research was on how to 'get' in the zone. I now believe that we are all in the zone and that the challenge is not getting into it; it is, in fact, staying there.

You may be surprised how many top athletes and leaders are terrified on the inside but have developed the ability to give off an entirely different perception. They have learnt how to manage their emotions to perform at their very best. The more they do it, the more natural it becomes.

When a sportsman is in the zone, time seems slower, they have clarity, and things just seem to bounce their way. As a business leader, you don't want to feel tense and stressed. This will cause anxiety and result in poor performance.

The zone is a place that every athlete wants to be in so he or she can compete at an optimum level. It has been described a number of ways. In his seminal work *Flow: The Psychology of Optimal Experience*, Mihaly Csikszentmihalyi proposes that people are happiest when they are in a state of *flow* – a state of concentration or complete absorption with the activity at hand and the situation. It is a state in which people are so involved in an activity that nothing else seems to matter.[8] Patsy Rodenburg, in her wonderful book *Presence,* refers to a similar place as 'Circle 2'. Second Circle presence is about being in the moment, and being in the moment keeps you open to change.[9]

When an athlete is in the zone, the subconscious takes over, and the athlete is playing on instinct. Things appear to be moving slower and the person is absolutely focused without the distraction of the conscious mind, allowing the conscious mind to focus on external tasks, limiting the amount of 'interference' from the athlete's inner critics.

Another key factor to consider when developing the ability to stay in the zone is how you perceive a threat. The bigger the threat, the more cortisol is released in your body. Cortisol is the stress hormone that helps protect you in danger, but it's not necessarily useful for high performance.

Research and neuroscientific evidence illuminate the idea of maintaining clarity and staying present, and you can use this information to your advantage. The Industrial Revolution gave rise to increased instances of diseases like cancer. The Digital Revolution is linked to the rise

8   Mihaly Csikszentmihalyi, *Flow: The Psychology of Optimal Experience* (New York: Harper & Row, 1990).

9   Patsy Rodenburg, *Presence: How to Use Positive Energy for Success* (New York: Penguin, 2009).

in mental health problems, which could be, in part, due to the sheer overwhelming volume of 'stuff' that we're bombarded with every day. People are constantly trying to keep up with the latest marketing tools or the latest social platform. Many younger people are obsessed with getting a certain number of followers and building their personal brand. There's something wonderfully freeing about having the capacity to just stand still, stand firm, and be resilient, like an immovable rock amidst the swirling tides of activity. Don't be afraid to take a step back and be mindful and present in the moment. Like Al Pacino says in *Any Given Sunday*, 'That's what living is, the six inches in front of your face...that's all there is.' You've got your targets, and you've got your plan. You're ready to start winning daily. For that to happen, you've got to stay absolutely present by removing the mist.

There are two types of mist: red and white. The red mist rolls in when you're angry, when you exert energy, or when you become frustrated. You don't think clearly, your temper's hot, and you're likely to lash out or make rash, heat-of-the-moment decisions. Athletes are familiar with the red mist, as is just about anyone trying to make it in the world today.

The white mist is what rolls in and obliterates the field or makes it hard for you to you to think logically or make sense of what's happening. You may feel mentally or physically paralysed, and this feeling is usually borne of a fear of failure. The more you stretch yourself outside of your comfort zone, the more you may encounter the white mist.

FIGHT OR FLIGHT

Think of it as fight or flight. The red mist triggers your fight response, and the white mist triggers your flight response.

On a physical level, managing the mist is about your ability to engage the parasympathetic nervous system when you're feeling under pressure or experiencing a stressful situation. You don't need to practise yoga, meditate, or become a mindfulness guru to live stress free. Integrating practical breathing techniques into your day will add huge benefits to your health, well-being, and performance.

You can achieve this through deep breathing, which you can do on the train, driving, or even in conversation. We'll discuss breathing later in this chapter. It will help you reduce stress in your life, decrease blood pressure, improve blood flow to your gut, and slow your heart rate.

This is particularly important post a tough exercise session, after a difficult negotiation, or during a stressful situation. This is when your heart is pumping blood hard using the sympathetic nervous system, which is responsible for your body's fight-or-fight response. It's what our ancestors relied on for sprinting away from danger or engaging in combat against a threat. When this happens, your pupils dilate, your heart rate increases, and your blood pressure rises. Your ability to transition to activating your parasympathetic nervous system will help you stay present, calm, and always ready. Your ability to self-regulate emotions is a competitive advantage.

The human brain doesn't distinguish between stressful situations. It just identifies a threat or stressor and responds accordingly. We are biologically designed to fight a stressor or flee from it. It doesn't matter whether you're putting on the eighteenth hole for the championship, about to give a keynote speech, or being confronted by a grizzly bear.

The emotional response to a threat happens in a nanosecond. In this situation, you could count to ten and wait for the mist to disappear, but in competitive sports or in the business world, ten seconds is the difference between winning and losing. The goal in a highly emotional situation is to focus your mind on managing your breathing and your posture. You can't control your emotions. It will only end in loss of control eventually.

Public speaking is an obvious example of a threat. I have learnt to enjoy public speaking, although my first experience was a disaster. I had a severe case of the white mist, frozen to the spot, suffocated by the breathing in my throat. The pace of my voice was fast, and I just wanted to get off the stage. I have developed a way to keep the fear in perspective. I do this by asking myself, 'What is the worst-case scenario?' and find I can usually live with whatever I identify. This technique helps me relax. My voice resonates better, and my speaking improves.

Like anything you do in life, practice plays an integral role in improving performance, but you have got to get out there in the first place and practise. Experience equals performance improvement. Development isn't confined to just theory and classroom training. It only accounts for ten per cent. The real learning takes place in the action. This book will equip you with ideas, models, and tools, but unless you practise them, they will have little effect on your performance.

If you suffer with the red mist or white mist, it is likely that you have a 'trigger' or 'button' that gets pulled or pushed. It could be an irrational response to something that is connected to the past, yet subconsciously, you make a link to it in the present. It could be the sound of a voice, the look of a person you meet, or the environment you are in. In therapy terms, this is referred to as *transference*. A simple example is how you may instantly warm to a person or perhaps take a disliking to them. You are effectively transferring a subconscious image from the past onto someone new and reacting the same way in the present. The same could be said of an experience you had as child, such as being made fun of in a reading class. This may cause you to behave a certain way, which could be entirely different from the person next to you, even though you are experiencing the same event. You may have difficulty making sense of these reactions. While this book is about taking action from the present towards the future – and is definitely not a book on therapy – we can all benefit with making sense of some deep-rooted experiences.

You've likely heard about elite warriors, snipers, and athletes who can shut out the chaos and calm themselves, achieving inner peace amidst a myriad of distractions. These are the most effective people within their fields. This ability is partly training, partly maturity, and partly due to their brain's development. Top-performing athletes, with the aid of sports psychologists, can enter a challenge state rather than a threat stance. In a threatened state, our bodies and brains get increasingly stressed, and we start to produce copious amounts of cortisol, which can be useful for short periods. But in a permanently threatened state, we quickly become ill or burn out. In 2015, research out of the University of California, Berkeley, has demonstrated that chronic stress generates long-term changes in the brain that lead to anxiety and mood disorders.[10]

According to research by Yale scientists, chronic stress leads to a loss of synaptic connections between brain cells, which could result in decreased brain mass in the prefrontal cortex – the part of your brain just behind the forehead that's responsible for regulating behaviour. In other words, stress literally shrinks the size of your brain.[11]

You only get one brain, and it's important that you look after it as best you can so it continues to serve you well.

During the history of humanity, the fight-or-flight response has kept our species alive, but now, in this modern world, this primitive instinct is being overworked. Having an understanding of how the brain functions will help you move into a controlled challenge state, which is a state of heightened awareness and clarity, rather than a threatened position. Once you manage to move into a challenge state, you'll be able to turn what could have been a disaster if the mist had rolled in, into an oppor-

---

10 Robert Sanders, 'New Evidence That Chronic Stress Predisposes Brain to Mental Illness,' *Berkeley News*, February 11, 2014, accessed October 10, 2018, http://news.berkeley.edu/2014/02/11/chronic-stress-predisposes-brain-to-mental-illness.

11 Bill Hathaway, 'Yale Team Discovers How Stress and Depression Can Shrink the Brain,' *Yale News*, August 12, 2012, accessed October 10, 2018, https://news.yale.edu/2012/08/12/yale-team-discovers-how-stress-and-depression-can-shrink-brain.

tunity. Elite athletes and business leaders have clarity and presence under pressure that allows logical, rational thought. This state also allows them to connect with their gut instincts and tap into their intuition, whereas in fight-or-flight mode, the mist would've clouded this connection.

THE MIST IN ACTION

The limbic system, often referred to as the 'chimp brain', is the part of your brain that reacts to the world around you reflexively and instantaneously in real time and without thought. For that reason, it gives off a true response to information coming from the environment. The limbic system is also the emotional centre, and it is from there that signals go out to various parts of your brain which in turn orchestrate your behaviours as they relate to emotions and your survival.

The key player in the limbic system is the amygdala, derived from the Latin word for almond, because of its shape. This tiny structure is involved in the processing of intense emotions, such as fear, and, as such, has been essential to our survival for millennia, responding instinctively to protect us when it perceives fear. This is when the red or white mist appears.

We've all done something that we've learnt to regret.

You've reacted to something and made a split-second decision without conscious thought in just 12 milliseconds, and later, when you had time to reflect, you thought, *What the hell was I thinking?* You weren't thinking. You were reacting instinctively, and this can serve you well when you're having to make quick-fire decisions. This happens because of the tiny but vastly complex system of structures that make up the limbic system and lie deep in the cerebral hemispheres. The limbic system links to the brain stem, which links to the higher-reasoning elements of the cerebral cortex, and together they help you carry out instinctive behaviours and manage emotions. The limbic system is also responsible for interpreting smells and linking them with memories and emotions. It reacts to your environment instinctively, without conscious thought, and determines your behaviour as it relates to your emotions.

Lots of things in your everyday life can cause the white mist to appear. It could be external stimuli like urgent work-related tasks that crop up: a client suddenly needs something, or perhaps you get a phone call from home that needs to be dealt with right away. Internal factors include your internal dialogues, feelings of inadequacy, or imposter syndrome.

Although our brain only makes up approximately two per cent of our body weight, it uses around 20 per cent of our energy. When you're operating in a threat state, you're under stress or in fight-or-flight mode, so your brain uses up to 100 times more energy. This is why, after those stressful days, you feel so drained and fatigued. In business, when this stress state occurs, you're often at your desk. As the pressure mounts, your body moves into fight-or-flight mode, releasing cortisol in conjunction with released adrenaline. As a result, your intellect drops as it relies on the chimp brain to focus solely on the danger, such as a sabre-tooth tiger. Your body recognises the feelings of stress, and to keep you prepared for rapid action, it mobilises stored carbohydrates and fats, and turns proteins into glucose. This allows the body to use the energy to sprint as fast as you can away from the threat or use the energy to fight it. However, in today's world, unlike our Palaeolithic ancestors, it's unlikely the glucose and fat will get burned up while you sit at your desk!

Even if you appear outwardly very fit, if you're constantly working under great stress and not burning off the additional energy regularly throughout the day, you could still have fatty deposits around your liver, and you may even notice stubborn fat around your midsection, despite regular exercise. This can put you at risk for a number of life-threatening diseases. There is nothing mentally tough about thriving on stress, mental toughness is defined by how you compose yourself and manage your emotions when triggered by stress.

In one of my workshops, I split the participants into two groups. I tell Group A to share their favourite hobbies with the other group – something they're really passionate about. I tell Group B they must make fun of Group A's hobbies for a full minute, even if they actually like those hobbies. Both groups are aware of one another's goals in this exercise. Group A starts off energised and engaged as they express their passions, but once Group B starts belittling or mocking those hobbies, the energy changes rapidly, and there's a lot of posturing and arm-crossing, with Group A participants animatedly defending their hobbies. Once the exercise is over, the feedback is always the same: though Group A knew the Group B participants were joking, they were still triggered into the mist, feeling aggressive with their hearts pounding and throats getting tight. Even when your prefrontal cortex, the conscious part of you, clearly tells you that what you're experiencing is an exercise, your instinctive brain still moves to fight mode. This demonstrates how challenging it can be to keep your composure when under pressure.

IDENTIFY YOUR TRIGGERS

Over the last 20 years, researchers and neuroscientists have made great strides understanding how the brain works and its effect on performance. However, we've discovered no more than one per cent of the secrets the immensely complex human brain holds. We do know enough to be able to make sense of the impact it has on performance across *The 4 Keys*. The way your brain works influences your business performance, how you engage with your loved ones, how you push your body and control your mindset, and your thoughts, feelings, and perceptions.

Different situations, roles, levels of competition, and types of stressors require different levels of mental toughness. Business leaders have to find ways to remain calm, because they experience similar stressors and challenges and their brains respond accordingly. As you start to recognise what pushes your buttons and brings about the red or white mist, you can prepare yourself to overcome the effects of that mist.

When you deliver a keynote speech, if you move into fight-or-flight response, the white mist will swoop in and hold you paralysed with fear. You get to your podium, look out, and can't see anything of the audience due to the white mist, or maybe it's only one or two people who really stand out. But you can learn to manage that mist, have clarity, see your audience, and communicate with them with confidence.

When you're free of the mist and have clarity, you project confidence and gravitas, so it goes beyond just having clear thought and being present in the moment. It also translates into how others perceive you when you're engaging with them. Clear the mist and get back on task by reminding yourself of your whys. Why are you writing that book, trying to make that deal, launching that website? Remind yourself of your vision.

You can project your stress and anxiety onto other people, and the reverse is also true. If you project calmness, relaxation, and confidence, you encourage others to feel the same way, which encourages them to trust and engage with you. If you're in a negotiation, for example, and you're in fight mode – the red mist – there's a good chance you'll put your negotiating partner into the same state, which is ultimately bad for both of you, as you'll end up locking horns.

What's your defence mechanism? Do you go into fight mode and experience the red mist? Or do you tend to withdraw and enter flight mode, with the white mist? Whichever is your go-to response, you need to identify what your triggers are. Where you feel confident and happy, where you're relaxed and enjoying yourself, that's your zone. Think about what throws you out of your zone. These are your triggers. With the athletes I coached, we'd do this same exercise to identify what their triggers were. It could be a coach, one of the other players, a particular topic of conversation, or something that happened out on the field. Once those triggers are made clear, you can think proactively and plan for them. Being prepared ensures that instead of getting lost in the mist, you remain focused and calm and don't lose your clarity. Remember, when you're approaching a sharp bend in the road, if you know it's coming, you can slow down in plenty of time and then accelerate through the bend rather than driving through fog, not seeing the bend until the last second, slamming on your brakes, and spinning out of control.

When you're under pressure, you'll either exert more energy as you try to force the situation, or you'll withdraw completely. Some people get overconfident when they get overexcited. That's because they're experiencing a rush of dopamine, which is the chemical associated with reward. This can lead them to take more risks as they crave more of the feelings associated with success, in which case they abandon their processes and systems that originally helped them to achieve that success. This, in turn, inevitably leads them to start to slip, in which case, they are enveloped in the white mist, and they withdraw, their focus switching from offence to defence. They doggedly defend what they achieved, and the memory of the feeling of successes fades, so their confidence drops. Then they stop taking action or become overly stressed. This is a turbulent, emotional rollercoaster.

Being consistent is a much better choice. The best sports teams, particularly in soccer or ice hockey, are consistent, whereas the teams who act sporadically and quickly get ahead early in the game are the ones that tend to get complacent and take their foot off the gas. They forget about their processes and systems and give their opponents an opportunity to mount a comeback.

Even if these feelings seem as if they are beyond your control, the challenge remains the same: stay present in the moment. Notice what's going on for you every day. Let your conscious mind influence the subconscious as you develop your self-management system, learn to slow down, and to manage the mist to retain your clarity. One of the best tools to help you is box breathing.

BOX BREATHING

Getting your breathing right is crucial. It improves your cognitive function, makes your vision sharper, decision-making easier, and enhances your listening skills. Even your voice projection changes when you engage in rhythmic breathing.

As a kid, I was in awe of people who could hold the attention of a room with nothing but their confident voice. Great leaders, actors, and athletes all have it. They are at ease with themselves, and they exude confidence. Roger Federer, Al Pacino, and President Obama all have that presence. Denzel Washington is known to take 40 deep breaths before a scene, slowing his breathing. Patsy Rodenburg, who is an amazing voice coach, works with actors and keynote speakers and teaches the importance of physiology – posture and breathing – and how getting some kind of rhythm going gives you clarity. You can achieve this clarity with box breathing. Box breathing is something you can do anywhere – in your car, backstage before a presentation, during exercise, and in the middle of a negotiation. It's easy, practical, and considered less woolly than meditating.

Box breathing, or square breathing, involves picturing a square. You can be anywhere, sitting or standing, with your hands on your lap or holding hands. Imagine that square. Breathe in through your nose, keeping your mouth closed, for a count of four. This is the first line that makes up the square. Hold that breath for four. That's the second line of the square. Breathe out for four to complete the third line, then hold your breath for a count of four to finish the square. Some people find holding the exhalation for a count of four challenging at first because they feel like they are suffocating. To begin with, repeat this sequence five times to get yourself into the rhythm and used to managing your breathing. Feel how it changes your gravitas, your listening skills, your clarity, and your composure.

BOX BREATHING

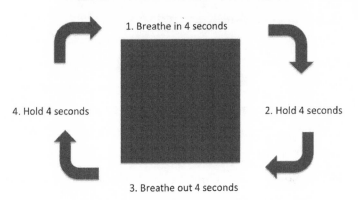

1. Breathe in 4 seconds

2. Hold 4 seconds

3. Breathe out 4 seconds

4. Hold 4 seconds

Patsy Rodenburg, the voice coach, calls it taking a belly breath. She likens it to a baby laying on its back. Babies are completely present and utterly connected with their world, and when you watch a healthy baby breathe, you'll see its belly rise and fall. As adults, when we go into flight mode, our breathing rises until we're breathing shallowly, from our necks, and it can feel like we're suffocating or unable to catch our breath as the white mist comes down. When we enter fight mode, our breathing is short and heavy and centred in the chest as the red mist descends. At these times, what elite actors, athletes, and leaders do, is take a deep belly breath, or a box breath, to compose themselves. This technique is also used by the military for special forces, like snipers who need to be utterly composed in high-stress situations and have optimal clarity to make their shot. Basketball players and other sportspeople do the same, calming themselves amidst all the chaos to score. At first, this technique may seem a little awkward, but as you practise it, it'll become second-nature.

Get used to taking those five controlled breaths whenever the need arises. You can use the box breath technique to get yourself into the right frame of mind to start your day off right (satisfying your mindset key), as part of your morning routine. Just take five box breaths every morning before you leave the house. Use it throughout the day whenever you feel like you need to decompress. You can also combine it with your post-workout stretch session to rid yourself of the stress you build up during a HIIT session (body key). Take your belly breaths when you're faced with a client or a colleague who infuriates you, and you'll be calm and composed, your intellect will kick back in, and you'll be back in the game and performing at your best. Do it before you go into a meeting or a busy room (your business key). Try taking just one or two box breaths before you say something rash to your partner or right before someone speaks who you know is going to press your buttons (relationship key).

Box breathing will engage the parasympathetic response and help to slow the heart rate and regulate the autonomic nervous system, getting you back to a more healthful state. No matter how fit you are, it's perfectly normal to experience the red and white mists, but you can prepare for them with methods such as box breathing to mitigate the effects.

My workshop participants find box breathing extremely powerful. On the retreat, we run several exercises to demonstrate how easy it is to engage the trigger of the fight-or-flight response and engage the sympathetic nervous system. In one particular exercise, everyone splits into pairs and shares their stories with one another, and the listeners practise their box breathing. Sometimes a person's story can make the listener feel uncomfortable, which can stimulate adrenaline and provoke the listener to want to voice an opinion or withdraw from the situation. Practising box breathing helps them be more present, and they may even ask a question or two. After the exercise, they talk about how their listening skills were heightened. Because they were so focused and present, they can recall large portions of the story they heard.

Whatever method you use to manage the mist, make sure you give it enough time to stick. Remember, the brain is malleable, and its neuroplasticity lets you forge new neural pathways via what are known as *synapses*. If you do something repeatedly for 20, 30, 60, or 90 days, you're strengthening the synapses over time, moulding your brain, and creating brand new neural pathways. The more you repeat these new patterns, the more the pathway you created becomes hardwired. What gets fired gets wired, and once it's wired, that behaviour will become habit. Repeating these new patterns is the basis for change. Thinking, *There's no way I can change*, reinforces that self-doubting belief and those established pathways in the brain. Change the narrative to, 'I know I can change. I might not change my personality, and the changes might not happen overnight, but I know I can change because my brain is malleable and I have the power to shape it.'

Calm the negative inner voice and begin the process of creating the new pathways that lead to meaningful change. Commit to it, stretch yourself, and consistently take action.

At this point, you've got your vision, you've made your game plan, you've got your processes for making sure you win daily, and you know how to compose yourself under pressure. Once you've learnt to manage the mist, the next step in realising your vision in four keys is making behavioural changes. In Part 3, 'Live Your Vision', you'll identify the changes you need to make, and how to make them to achieve your vision.

PART III

LIVE YOUR VISION

CHAPTER 8

———

EMBRACE CHANGE

It is not the strongest of the species that survives, nor the most intelligent that survives. It is the one that is most adaptable to change.

—CHARLES DARWIN

I enjoy variety, and I get excited by change. If I'm working with an organisation and they change their systems, I can cope with that and I embrace it – I'm not stuck in my ways. Some people are more resistant to change, particularly within organisations. If you change their PC, the processes they follow, or their environment, you immediately throw them into fight-or-flight mode because they see these changes as threats. They close down or withdraw, and their performance suffers. However, there are still things that hold me back at a deeper level and that I struggle to change. I know that this happens at an emotional level.

This is true for everyone. At an emotional level, we are all resistant to change, but once we recognise that resistance and make up our minds to do something about it – despite the emotions it might invoke – we can make real progress towards achieving our objectives in *The 4 Keys*. Keep in mind that resistance to change in one key can affect your performance in another key because they are all interrelated. For example, if you are struggling in your relationship key, it will have an effect on your business.

One of these things came to light as a minor epiphany during a conversation with my wife. She had contracted viral meningitis, which became the catalyst for our separation. She was in the hospital for ten days. I don't have a problem with hugging friends and family when I greet them. In most situations, I'm a friendly, tactile guy. But as I said earlier, I really struggled with dealing with people who were ill, injured, or upset. It wasn't intentional, but I couldn't embrace or connect with them in those situations. In those circumstances, I wanted to express my sympathy or show empathy, but I just froze up. I couldn't show my wife the sympathy she needed during that difficult time. She said that I was 'emotionally challenged', and I think there was some truth to that observation. But my wife's words made me realise something inside me needed to change. I knew this would take deeper work and reflection and that dealing with issues like this are where a coach could help. Of course, if you have deep-seated issues that cannot be resolved by working with a coach, you may consider therapy. That type of consultation may have been associated with weakness in the past, but more and more, people are realising that therapy can be truly beneficial for people who are successful in life yet require a little extra help to reach their full potential.

For myself, I recognised my aversion to empathising with others was holding me back in my relationships, and I worked hard to examine and overcome this behaviour. This was a change I needed to make because I became very much aware of how it was affecting my personal relationships.

Issues like this don't just affect your personal relationships. If you can't empathise with a family member, you probably can't empathise with customers, colleagues, or your team, and that will affect your business and your career. If you're with a co-worker or a client who's having problems at work or at home and they become upset, you may not be able to offer them the emotional support they need.

Likewise, if you are unable to manage unhealthy personal relationships, you may have found yourself in a dysfunctional relationship that you knew was not healthy for you, but the pain of leaving that person might have seemed worse than the pain you were already in, so you avoided the pain and found comfort in the pain. You may also find it difficult to deal with unhealthy business relationships. If you've ever had a particularly difficult colleague or client, you may have managed the situation similarly. By avoiding the conflict, thus refusing to acknowledge and deal with the situation, however, you are merely prolonging the pain.

Looking back, I admire my wife for moving out. It took huge amounts of courage to leave with the kids and give our relationship the space it required. Although, at the time, my wife was adamant our marriage was over and there was no going back. However, had she stayed and tried to make it work, I fear the situation would have become more emotional and toxic.

I'm pleased to say that due to my wife giving us the space and due to both of us making the situation as amicable as possible for the children's sake, we have come a long way. As of writing this book, we still live separately, but our relationship has improved, creating a much better environment in which our children may thrive. The long-term benefits massively outweighed the short-term pain.

Change can be very fast, too fast for some people. In business, there is constant change, and this can cause you anxiety; furthermore, if you have employees and they feel they cannot keep up with the pace, they will struggle to execute on the strategy. For the most part, your team will understand your vision at an intellectual level, but to fully engage and make the necessary changes, they need to emotionally connect with it and feel it the way you do. When change is asked of us, we want to know, 'What's in it for us?' Then we are far more likely to embrace the change.

You may be someone who embraces change and enjoys the variety – perhaps you're happy to make a few mistakes along the way and learn from them – or you may be someone who won't even attempt to change until you are sure you can deal with it and therefore prefer a clear framework and certainty. Some people naturally embrace the unknown, while others do not without full awareness of the potential outcomes. Of course, there are varying degrees of a person's willingness to accept change, and you may respond differently under certain circumstances.

Athletes go through change during their careers. They have to learn to adapt to new rules and regulations. They are given new equipment designed to enhance their performance. In some cases, it may have a detrimental effect on performance in the short term. Very often, an athlete will have to change their technique to reach their own vision. The same adaptations are required in business, where an industry, technology, and clients' needs are always in flux. Being open to change will benefit you in your work and may also require a mindset shift. It means being brave – brave enough to change your behaviours and embrace change in order to move closer to achieving your vision.

My dad loved golf and got down to a respectable handicap. I remember my dad talking about Nick Faldo and how, in the mid-1980s, Faldo took action to make himself a better player by changing his swing. Initially, Faldo's performance dropped, but eventually, his swing became more efficient, and he accomplished his goal. Apparently, he hit 1,500 practice balls a day. The practising paid off, and in 1989 he won his second major tournament, the Masters. Faldo went on to win a number of other tournaments in 1989, including the Volvo PGA Championship and the Dunhill British Masters. Had he not made the brave decision and taken the risk to make the changes to his swing, he may never have won those competitions. Change requires action and is likely to feel clunky at first when developing new habits.

BEHAVIOURS THAT HOLD YOU BACK

I've never worked with an athlete, business leader, or organisation that has achieved their goal without embracing change. It's crucial. None of us are perfect, and we all have things to work on and improve so we can serve others and ourselves better.

Think of leaders who didn't look back and didn't play it safe yet made real change happen. It may not have made sense at the time. Henry Ford said, 'If I asked people what they wanted, they would have said faster horses.' It takes vision, purpose, and also an element of risk and a willingness to change to see your goals through.

Would Apple be where it is today if Steve Jobs hadn't embraced failure? Would Blockbuster still exist if it had been prepared to move outside its comfort zone? Would Netflix have taken off if it hadn't changed its business model?

Kodak is a prime example of a business that couldn't embrace change because of their culture and the way they typically behaved. The company developed the first digital camera, but they were so fearful that it would negatively impact their share in the camera film industry that they didn't release it. Successful business leaders understand the necessity to consistently disrupt their businesses and processes with one eye on the future, and the same applies to us personally. We need to continually disrupt ourselves, asking, 'Is the way I'm operating helping me move towards my vision?'

Even though you've got your vision, you're clear about your purpose, you've got your 90-Day Reset with your 30- and 60-day benchmarks in place, and you understand how to win daily, unless you're willing to make and embrace necessary changes, it's highly unlikely you'll succeed.

The environment you've grown up in has shaped you and your behaviour. You may be wired – due to your upbringing, your experiences, or perhaps even your genetics – to respond to things a certain way. You may know in your mind that you need to change direction in your life, or change something in your business, yet you may be hesitant due to this 'wiring'. On the other hand, there are people who react quickly and spontaneously to change, and while that can help them achieve their goals, it can also be a hindrance if not tempered with careful observation and consideration.

Humans don't stand still; we continue to evolve. We have to keep moving forward, and to do that successfully, we need to embrace change. This is a pivotal moment where you have to decide whether what you've been doing up to now has been truly serving you. Whatever behaviours have bought you here, will they get you where you need to go across *The 4 Keys*? This is about more than simply deciding you need to change your business systems or products. What are you going to change in yourself that's going to make an impact across all the keys?

START SMALL AND MIND THE RISKS

As a business psychologist, I look at ways to improve a business' structure and how to create behavioural and mindset changes. These changes involve an element of risk, as does every change. Therefore, the best way to implement these changes is to formulate a plan. Start small and be mindful of the attached risks. Making sudden or significant changes can be painful or uncomfortable, so test the waters and get yourself used to change with manageable shifts.

In my experience, children who grow up experiencing lots of changes, like moving houses regularly, or who have their routines mixed up frequently may grow into adults who can more easily embrace change. We moved around a lot when my children were young, and now my daughter is very open to change. This led me to believe that a child who grew up with an unwavering routine and utterly stable life isn't likely to adapt to changes so easily when they mature. However, a child who grew up experiencing lots of changes could grow to react quite differently to structure and routine, perhaps by rebelling.

Think about your own past and your relationship with change. Do you crave predictability and structure? If you're someone who doesn't like to make changes, ask yourself whether the routines and behaviours you're clinging to are really serving you. Even the resistance to change is a behavioural pattern, so consider whether it is of benefit or is detrimental to you. Has it held you back? Have you missed out on opportunities? Do you have regrets? Take the emotion out of the equation and look at it objectively. Would it have served you better if you'd been a little braver and made those changes? Based on those answers, do you need to start thinking differently to achieve your vision? Now is the time to start being braver and making small changes to see what happens.

Think of a time when you've set a goal for yourself, yet excuses manifested themselves that prevented you from achieving it. For some reason, you didn't execute on that goal, and you don't know why. You may have put the brakes on and started making excuses for why you didn't need to keep working towards that outcome anymore. Your internal voice popped up and convinced you that you didn't need to make that much revenue or that your relationship is really okay.

That voice, and the thoughts or excuses your brain produces to put the brakes on and resist the changes you're making, can sabotage your progress. Prepare yourself for them by imagining them before they occur. This allows you to think about them, see them for what they are, and negate them before they crop up. Then you'll have time to prepare for them and have a plan to manage them if they try to sabotage your game plan. Think back to the driving analogy – preparing yourself for these thoughts means you know they are ahead, just like that sharp bend in the road, so you can navigate them safely. Know they're coming, focus on your objective and the why behind it, and then respond to them more mindfully so you can prevent them from derailing your progress.

Say at one point you were trying to develop a better emotional connection with your partner. Perhaps that relationship wasn't going so well, and there was tension between the two of you. The first, small step you could have taken would be to establish which behaviours were working against you in building that desired emotional connection. One detrimental behaviour might be that you were not always present. Maybe when you were having conversations, you weren't really listening. Instead, you were glancing at your phone, watching the telly, or your mind was on work. Your partner sensed this behaviour, and it prevented you from connecting with them.

Another behaviour that might sabotage your emotional connection could be doing or saying things that don't align with your partner's motivations. For example, if one of their key motivators is acts of service, they may be motivated by you going out of your way to do something nice for them, such as cooking a nice meal or pitching in to help out with the chores. If you are unfamiliar with key motivators and how they affect your relationships,

I recommend the book *The 5 Love Languages*.[12] On the other hand, your key motivators might be touch and intimacy, so there is a disconnect in how you relate to one another emotionally.

If you've ever gotten an unexpected response to an act that you offered with the best intentions, you know what I'm talking about. I recall coming home from work and giving my wife a hug from behind while she was preparing dinner and expecting a certain response. Instead, she was disappointed. What she really wanted from me was to take the kids out for a couple of hours so she could enjoy cooking the meal or work on her business undisturbed. At the time, I was confused by this reaction, but I came to realise that I was not considering her key motivators, which were completing her work so we could both enjoy a relaxing evening together.

Those key motivators are what you need to identify and seek to adapt to, and that means changing your behaviour. If your partner was busy cooking a big meal for the family, and you lovingly put your arms around her while she's chopping vegetables for salad, she might be very irritated, thinking, *What, now? Can't you see how busy I am, and why can't you help me?* Whereas if she did the same to you, you'd be likely to drop whatever you're doing and enjoy the intimacy. Some people prefer to have all the chores

---

12   Gary Chapman, *The 5 Love Languages: The Secret to Love that Lasts* (Chicago: Northfield, 2015).

done, enjoy the meal, relax, and then get intimate, while others are more spontaneous and couldn't care less about these details if there's an opportunity for a loving connection. That's where the misalignment and the disconnect happens, and where the opportunity for change appears. You can talk to your partner about these differences, but if you truly want to create a better emotional connection, one or both of you needs to recognise the other's key motivators and be willing to change their behaviour.

This sounds easy in theory, but in practice, making behavioural changes can be very difficult. Harvard professor Bob Kegan, author of *Immunity to Change,* asks, 'What do you fear if you do the exact opposite of the behaviours that are working against your improvement goals?'[13] You may identify an improvement goal that's linked to your 90-Day Reset, but you continue with your usual behavioural pattern. This is your brain protecting you from changing your habits, what Professor Kegan refers to as your *immunity.* So you have one foot on the accelerator towards your vision and completing your 90-Day Reset, and then the brakes get slammed by your subconscious. Your brain is trying to protect you, but in effect, it's sabotaging your efforts.

Consider the emotions you would feel if you did the oppo-

---

13   Robert Kegan and Lisa Laskow Lahey, *Immunity to Change: How to Overcome It and Unlock the Potential in Yourself and Your Organization* (Boston: Harvard Business School, 2009).

site of those behaviours that don't serve you. Ask yourself, *What do I fear?* In the example about connecting better with your partner, you would put your affectionate desires aside and help out with chores, take turns cooking dinner, or cook dinner together.

I tried this exercise myself: What would happen if I were able to be supportive of others who were experiencing anguish, pain, or sorrow? What if I could empathise with them or offer them sympathy? What was I afraid of? I had to really think about this question and respond honestly. The answer surprised me. I was literally terrified of becoming uncontrollably emotional myself, like in my recurring dream. I feared that if I put my arms around somebody who needed my support, I'd end up sobbing, detracting from their needs and making the issue all about me. While this may sound silly, it's not something I could 'just get over' or change overnight, because remember, what gets fired gets wired, and this response had been hardwired in my brain over the course of years, so it seemed impossible to flip a switch and unwire the behaviour.

Likewise, even though you know it would be beneficial to your relationship, subconsciously, you may be worried that if you go out of your way to please your partner by doing the chores, she'll reject you or not fully appreciate it. This behaviour can affect each of your keys. For example, one of your objectives in the 90-Day Reset may be to give up alcohol for three months, you may fear the reaction of your friends and colleagues if you order a soda water while they're all enjoying beers. Do you think they might ridicule you? Will they reject your friendship if you don't drink alcohol? Or do you maybe think you won't enjoy yourself as much? It seems silly when you put it that way, yet these are the kinds of underlying thoughts that can permeate your brain when you're trying to make a positive change, and they can sabotage your progress. Think about what's preventing you from changing your behaviour: Is it real or imagined, logical or far-fetched?

Recently, my oldest daughter came to me upset because her grandparent's dog, with whom she had a close bond, had been put to sleep. I saw this as a great opportunity to offer my child some comfort and to practise being emotionally present. Knowing how I feel about offering sympathy, her initial reaction as I approached was, 'No, don't hug me,' but I did. Hugging someone who is emotionally vulnerable once stirred up unpleasant memories for me, but by forcing myself to do it, I've created new pathways in my brain that experience this behaviour in a more positive way. If you have behaviours that you're trying to change, consciously force yourself to respond differently, even if it goes against your natural inclination. Try doing this for one month and see how you begin to change your natural reactions.

You have to be brave and make a concerted effort to change the behaviours that don't serve you or support your four key visions. At the same time, you have to be careful not to force yourself to change too drastically or quickly, as this can push you into fight-or-flight mode. A sudden, dramatic change can unearth firm resistance and make you feel threatened. However, if you are committed to embracing change and you recognise these old behaviours are damaging you and holding you back from your desired outcomes, then you've got to be courageous and press forward using this practical approach.

By examining your behaviours and asking yourself questions about why you cling to them, you can see all these unconscious fears manifesting themselves. Then you can see them for what they are and manage them with small steps. If I tell you to just man up and make the changes necessary to improve your plight, you'll most likely be more resistant. However, if I ask you to just give it a try with one of those behaviours for a couple of weeks – like cook dinner or hug someone when you see they're upset or switch to soda water – you'll be more willing to take that step because it's not so overwhelming. You don't have to do it all the time, every day, but you can test it out, and even if you don't always succeed immediately, it's likely that you'll see that your fears are unfounded. Your fears, at this point, are merely assumptions that need to be tested. Once you've done it for two weeks, you can do it for another two, or a month, or your whole 90 days. Stretching yourself isn't just about setting stretch targets. Real results come from recognising your behaviours, getting out of your comfort zone, and changing them.

The examples I've chosen here are emotive and body ones, and it may be that your relationships and health are fine, but that it's your mindset or your business that needs help. These same techniques can be applied to any of *The 4 Keys*. Remember, too, that if your relationship is struggling, it's impacting your business, your mindset, and your physical health – whether or not you realise it. Similarly, anything out of balance in any one of *The 4 Keys* will have a negative impact on the others, so it's vital to start working through this system so that you can move towards making your vision a reality.

Einstein said that repeating the same pattern over and over again, expecting a different result, was the definition of insanity. So why would you continue to repeat those same behaviours knowing that the outcome won't help you? If you're struggling, remind yourself of your why, and get back to testing out those changes. This is not a skill that you learn, but rather a behavioural change, and mastering the ability to change your behaviours will have a dramatic impact on your four keys success.

EMBRACE FAILURE

Failure is success if we learn from it.

—MALCOLM FORBES

You've recognised your fear of change, and now you're going to challenge your assumptions. You might still procrastinate a little, thinking, *Well, I want to test these assumptions, but I'm just not brave enough.* After all, you could fail. That's okay. You can handle this, but you have to prepare yourself to embrace failure.

When it comes to implementing something new, even though people understand the theory and the process, they freeze. As head coach of Team GB, I saw this behaviour on a regular basis. I'd drill the team on the changes and get the entire team onboard. They'd all understand it and openly converse about this new thing. Then we'd go to the rink to practise it, and they'd do the opposite of what we'd just talked about, or they'd freeze and not play with their usual freedom. This is the point in sports at which you'll often see coaches start screaming at their players because they're frustrated and can't understand why the team can't do the play they just finished talking about. Then, the coach will call their players in, lose their patience, shout, and send them back out. Once again, the team doesn't get the play. There's a behaviour of fearing failure that's working against them. I recognised that I and my team had to change the way we played, and one of those changes was getting comfortable with the opposing teams being close to us, particularly when we were up against a superior force.

In hockey, you're generally trying to keep the puck away from your opponent. It's not comfortable to have an opponent leaning on you, but one of the big differences between average players and elite ones is that those players at the top of their game are completely comfortable with letting another player stand on their shoulder, whilst they remain able to protect the puck. These players let their opponents stay on their shoulder, and they're essentially standing between that opponent and the puck. With your opponent in that position, you have the opportunity to pick and roll off that person and make a better play. My team understood that concept and the reasons behind it on an intellectual level. They got it. But when we went out onto the rink, they were fearful. They wouldn't get close to their opponents. They'd leave this big gap that allowed the other player to poke-check and steal the puck. I asked them, 'What's the worst-case scenario here?' It transpired that their main concern was that if they got too close to their opponent, that player would be able to steal the puck, get a breakaway, and score, so I said, 'But that's what's happening anyway because you're not doing it. So what's the *real* worst-case scenario? What if they do score?'

One of them said, 'Well, coach, you'd bench me, and if it kept happening, you'd drop me.'

I replied, 'Well, if you won't execute the play, I'll bench you. But you're not executing the play because you're afraid of getting benched. So what's the worst-case scenario if I bench you?'

'I don't get to play for Great Britain.'

'Worst-case scenario?'

'I don't go to the tournament.'

I said, 'Let's put that into perspective. What would you do if you didn't go to the tournament?'

'I'd just keep playing hockey.'

Once they relaxed and got that perspective, they were able to embrace the play and the prospect of failure. I'd take it a step further and build up their confidence to fail, saying, 'You're going to go out there and fail as hard as you can. Get so close to that player that you fail – and fail hard. Go into him, get really close, and see how many times you fail. And remember, the worst-case scenario really isn't that bad. If the other player steals the puck, knocks you over, or hits you, you'll still play hockey, and you'll live to fight another day, so embrace the failure.'

It worked. I can clearly remember the look of intensity on his face as that player, the one who was afraid of being benched or dropped, went all out to make that play. You may experience the same frustrations with your teams in your business. Or perhaps you're acting this way yourself? Don't let your way of thinking hold you back.

Failure can mean different things to different people. Do people with a winning mindset simply not fear failure? I don't think so. Everyone has something that they are threatened by at some point. As discussed earlier, we are biologically designed to detect danger. It's how top performers channel their fear that gives them an edge. They tend to thrive on the pressure. Roger Bannister breaking the four-minute mile, Tiger Woods dominating at golf (and making a comeback in 2017 after several spinal operations and a messy time in the press), and Michael Jordan are great examples of athletes who thrive under pressure.

I have spoken to hundreds of top performers who say they are driven to succeed *because* of the fear of failure. The idea of actually failing is enough for them to do whatever it takes to succeed. However, these types often become over-stressed and get the red mist. This can cause them to 'slam on the brakes' to stay in control, therefore becoming counterproductive. I have also observed and interviewed people who will not take on a challenge if they believe the goal is unachievable. They appear to avoid any possibility of failure by not even taking on the challenge in the first place. They say, 'Well, if I can't win, what is the point?' I have witnessed this attitude in many business owners who struggled to adapt to new ways of doing business. The point is, how will you learn if you don't take a risk? Any type of decision making is going to involve some degree of risk.

There are also many people out there who simply don't believe in themselves. They suffer from limiting beliefs and withdraw from situations, usually suffering with the white mist rather than just going for it to see what happens. They *could* embrace the learning experience rather than focusing on the end result.

Deep down, we all want to win. It is in our nature, whether you believe it or not. If you have the choice of taking first place or second, you'll take first place. Even if you're one of those people who feel guilty when beating the other person, it still feels good to win. To be truly successful, you will have to accept failure as a possibility and find a way to let go of any fear. Whenever there is a failure, there is a learning opportunity, which means there is always success. The other important point is that when we accept failure as a possibility and put it into perspective, we relax more, achieve clarity, and are more able to take advantage of the opportunities in front of us.

Look at yourself and figure this out: What are the things you need to fail hard at? What failures do you need to embrace to change your detrimental behaviours? If you're procrastinating or dithering, ask yourself what the worst-case scenario is and if it's really that bad.

DERAILED BY EGO

One of my fears was speaking in front of a camera. I have an online product, and launching my YouTube channel was a pretty important step in my business. If you asked me to step in at the last second and deliver a keynote to a stadium packed with 5,000 people, I'd do it without a second thought. But put me in front of a camera with nobody else around, and I would freeze. Many of these fears relate to my ego, with questions like, 'What if I deliver this message on video, post it on LinkedIn, and nobody likes it? What if people think I'm trying too hard or I'm disingenuous?' For me, it's my ego and concerns over my social status that are slowing me down. This is an example of having one foot on the accelerator towards my goal at an intellectual level, consciously knowing it would be good for my business, and then putting on the brake at a subconscious and emotional level.

It is the same situation for many business leaders – their fears are related to their ego and status. By failing hard and embracing failure, you'll be able to go for it. Just like the player I mentioned earlier who got really tight on his opponent, made the perfect play, and did it over and over again. Then, following his example, the whole team was inspired to do the same. As mentioned before, our team mantra was 'Playing safe is risky.' Remember, you need to be on the offence. For me, I'm going all out on the offence with my online presence. I'm tackling it head-on, prepared to fail and embrace that failure, so I can bring my authentic self to everything I do.

Ego both helps and hinders. If you look at anybody who is at the top of their field – elite athletes, musicians, actors, and business leaders – their ego is driving them to succeed. This is a useful, healthy manifestation of ego. However, when your ego consumes you, toxic, damaging behaviour begins to manifest, and you start to lose your purpose.

This happened to me in a big way while I was coaching Team GB. At the time, I was living my why, building a high-performance culture, and serving the players. In 2011 and 2013, we won the Pool B championships and were thriving. In 2014 we got into the top eight countries again, and I decided I wanted to play. I'd never played in Pool A, and I told them I wanted to get myself in shape and play the next year. The idea was for me to step down as head coach and let the assistant coach step up. The leadership agreed, and a few of the players liked the idea, with some saying, 'Yeah, we're missing a few defence-men.' My wife tried to tell me she had doubts, but I was too focused on the try-outs. My ego was taking over, and I had forgotten my purpose. Instead, I was focused on serving my passion instead of my team.

Within 24 hours, I'd gone from head coach to player, and from the outside, it looked really bad – like I'd selected myself, even though I hadn't. I went from being the coach who took the team and made history to the old guy who is only on the team because he'd chosen himself. There was a fair amount of backlash as the story went across Facebook and other social media. I stayed on the team and played in the world championships. I fulfilled one of my dreams – to play in Pool A. I remember playing against Slovakia, and we lost with 30 seconds to go. We got relegated.

At the time, I thought, rather unpleasantly, that we were on such an amazing trajectory under my leadership that we would've stayed in Pool A and would have created a better legacy if I'd still been in charge. But I selfishly chose to serve my passion instead of my purpose. Now, although I've apologised to my team, I have to live with that legacy. With my ego overriding my sense of purpose,

I felt like I'd been selfless as a leader and a coach, and I thought it was my turn. But it wasn't. I took the place of someone who could've had a completely different experience, and that could have resulted in the whole team having a different experience. I should have listened to my gut or gone to my own coach and asked for advice but, caught up in my passion, I had lost my purpose.

Ego can be a useful tool, or it can be a hinderance that gets in the way of the legacy you want to create. What legacy do you want to leave behind? How can you inspire others to be the best version of themselves through your own behaviours and by embracing change? How are you affecting other people and their experiences? Are you being true to yourself at the same time? Are you being your authentic self while serving your purpose?

When you're making important decisions, step back and examine your situation. This is a good time to practise box breathing, get clear on your purpose, remember your why, and ask yourself if your behaviours and choices are truly serving you. Pause, breathe, relax, and refocus. Whether you're thinking as a business leader, as a wife, a husband, or a coach, or thinking for your own physical and mental health, taking that time to breathe and reflect can help you make the best possible choices. Those choices can have lasting effects on your life and your legacy.

A CASE STUDY IN FEAR, EGO, AND CHANGE

A business leader I worked with wanted to scale his business. His desired 90-day outcome was to delegate more work to his staff. With coaching, he recognised that certain behaviours were not serving him towards that purpose. He'd participate in every conference call. He'd go out with his sales manager to meet with every big client. He'd bypass his sales manager and try to coach other employees. Once we identified the behaviours that weren't serving him, I asked him what he most feared if he did the opposite. He was afraid that his staff wouldn't be able to cope with the added responsibilities and that his business performance would suffer. Maybe the staff wouldn't get coached properly or wouldn't develop adequately if he didn't run the workshops. He was also afraid he wouldn't be perceived as the leader and that his status would drop and that his revenue would decline.

I reminded him that his business already wasn't growing, and he wasn't able to scale. On top of his business issues, he didn't have enough time with his family. Yet, the things he was already doing were working against his outcomes of scalability, delegation, and increased free time. He was afraid that the business' performance and his status would drop. I reminded him that performance already wasn't improving and was likely to drop. Feedback from his team told me that instead of them seeing him as a leader to be respected, he was perceived as someone who constantly undermined them. He had one foot on the accelerator and one on the brakes, so thanks to his ego, he wasn't getting anywhere.

I suggested he try making some behavioural changes for a month. Yes, there was some risk involved – he may lose a client, his team may not have the right training, and his revenue may drop a bit, so we had to be mindful of that, but the test was only for a month. We agreed that he wouldn't attend any conference calls or sales meetings, and he wouldn't get involved with coaching his team. Part of the test also required him to start thinking about the future of his business, where he wanted it to be, and who his successor would be.

As a result of this test, the engagement scores increased. People felt more relaxed and less pressured. The sales manager felt like he had real ownership and began to develop as a leader himself. The business owner was exponentially more productive in driving the business forward because he had more time to plan, find new clients, identify new markets, and shape the future of his company. He created a plan that let him feel like he was totally in control yet allowed him to get home to his family at a reasonable time every evening. His business improved, and that had a distinctly positive impact on the other three keys. He just needed to be brave enough to take that leap for a month.

With his personal relationships he'd liked to be in control, booking the holidays and pressuring his kids to perform well. He'd done it with the best of intentions, but he'd always felt like he didn't have enough time and like his family didn't appreciate or respect him. As we were working through his business key, he had his own epiphany and realised he didn't have to be in control all the time at home either. His relationships improved, and he achieved balance.

When you're looking to change something, especially behaviours and habits, consider the following steps:

1. Ask yourself: What do you want to improve?
2. Align it to your desired outcome from your 90-Day Reset.
3. Now ask:
   - What behaviours are working against your desired outcome?
   - What do you fear if you do the exact opposite of those behaviours?
   - Are those fears just assumptions that will potentially get in your way of achieving your vision and living your purpose?
   - What is the worst-case scenario?

4. Put it into perspective.
5. Take action.

Working through the above steps requires dedication to values: do the work, no excuses, always ready, speak the truth.

CHAPTER 9

———

LEAVE YOUR LEGACY

All good men and women must take responsibility to create legacies that will take the next generation to a level we could only imagine.

—JIM ROHN

You've identified the results you want, the behaviours you need to change to get there, and you know how to make those changes. You've got your desired outcomes, and you've turned those into SMART objectives, and now you're really getting into your 90-day game plan. You're seriously thinking about doing the work, what it will mean for you, and what it'll do for others. You're considering how you're going to inspire others to be the best versions of themselves by doing this work.

You can make the greatest impact through your actions. There's no need to start telling people that you're following this 90-day game plan and explain *The 4 Keys*. While there's nothing wrong with that – and it's great for my business if you *do* – if you really want to inspire others and make a positive impact on those around you, do it by just doing the work.

If you do choose to explain the game plan to someone, think ahead about how you're going to do this. One of my clients explained the programme to his wife. Then he told her, while they were in bed, that she was one of his four keys. Understandably, she freaked out, thinking she had unwittingly become some kind of experiment. We'd already spoken in our group about not doing that very thing and just taking action instead, but the man was making great progress and wanted to talk about it to the person closest to him.

Go into this process purposefully, with a willingness to serve others and not just yourself. Do the work, and others will see the changes you've wrought and will experience the benefits, as will you. You'll be surprised to find that people around you, as you go through your programme, will see the changes that you're making and will be inspired to make health, mindset, business, and relationship changes themselves.

My wife told me how much of a better father I am to Izzie, Freya, and Harry. I was surprised. I have always thought of myself as a good father, but Lucie's perception is her reality. She saw a shift in me, and on reflection, I understood what she meant. It was the 'always ready' value being applied. I'm not as fatigued or distracted. I am far more present and active with my kids. I have a different type of energy about me, and I feel like I am thriving and enjoying my children much more.

This happens with every group I work with, without the participants explaining the details to their friends, families, or colleagues, or even sharing the fact that they're in the plan.

Now it's your turn. Take everything you've learnt so far and refine it into your 90-Day Reset. Whether you've read the book cover to cover or just skimmed it up to this point, it's vital that you now get really clear on the programme and look at it as a legacy. It's not just about you. It's about the impact you have on those around you and how you make them feel through your actions.

What do you want to leave behind? For me, it's not just about making sure my loved ones are financially secure when I'm gone, although that plays a significant role. Remember, my dad lost everything, so he had nothing to leave his family. It's more about values – the foundations and stories that shape who you are, and how you manage them to be your best self. My dad's legacy to me was his optimism, which I believe pulled me through some of my most difficult times. My parents didn't teach me the core values I needed to succeed in business, body, relationships, and mindset, so I ended up repeating negative patterns for many years until I discovered *The 4 Keys* and learnt how to change my behaviours. I want to be remembered for my values and how they manifested themselves in behaviours that made people happy and inspired them to pursue their own visions. Jock, my mentor, had a strong set of values, and those are still ingrained in me. My mother's unconditional love still motivates me and gives me the confidence I need to believe in myself, always, and persevere.

Because of their values, behaviours, and legacies, I'm always conscious of how I portray myself to my children. I want to instil in them a fundamental set of values that set them in good stead for the rest of their lives. I praise them when I think they're doing well, and I let them know when something isn't appropriate and when they need to rethink it. My eldest, Izzie, is a remarkable young woman. I'm so proud of her, and she has a good set of values.

Your legacy can extend beyond your family to your employees and colleagues too. At Jock's funeral, it was clear to see just how many people he'd inspired in his lifetime.

Remember that you have the power to rewrite or break any pattern that isn't serving you. You can choose to make new patterns that help you be a better spouse, parent, or leader. You can make a fresh start at any point, and taking that action with a 90-day game plan will help you transform your business, your body, your relationships, and your mindset, and you'll keep on reaping the rewards long after the 90 days are up.

The 4 Keys have been tried and tested, and what started with a group of just five people continues to grow and reach people across the world. Recently, an online client of mine posted on LinkedIn that I was one of the most motivational and inspiring people he's ever come across, and that I've changed his life profoundly. I haven't even met this man, but he's done the online programme and is experiencing great success. I'm not bragging. I'm telling you that it is within your power to have this kind of impact on the lives of others. *Do the Work. No excuses. Speak the truth. Always ready.* Focus on *The 4 Keys* and make small steps every day. Once you start making these changes, you're going to see how you inspire others to make the changes too.

I'm not preaching. I'm a guy facing the same challenges

as you – just like all my clients, my participants in the 90-day game plan. We're not bragging about fancy cars or living in mansions. We're just doing the work, like you. We're ambitious. We want to be the best versions of ourselves. We're not perfect, but we're getting better every day.

Most of the people who enter *The 4 Keys* programme share similar values. We're not gregarious or out drinking every night. We're not ostentatious with our wealth. We're just normal folks with similar interests and aligned values. One of our group members asked if anyone would be interested in meeting up in London to go for a run. That's fun for us, and that's what our community is like. One of the guys in the group is a former England rugby player, and the programme has changed his life in many ways. Every time someone new joins our group, he says, 'Just be ready for the results, because it will be insane.' It's true, too, for everybody who commits and does the work.

Some people come into this programme thinking that it's purely about growing their business, and they buy into that aspect. Then they realise it's not really about that – or at least not *just* about that. Yes, we're all focused on growing our businesses, but we're also growing and thriving in the other three keys, and our businesses are thriving because of that.

Whether you've worked really hard through the exercises in this book or you've read it in one fell swoop and are just getting started, be sure to execute and take time to review. Reflect on your changes, your work, and your progress, and hold yourself accountable. Embrace the failures and celebrate the successes.

If you don't have a coach already, get one. The right coach will be as important to your business as your accountant. A coach will hold you accountable. Join our online programme or our Facebook group. Drop me an email.

Record your journey as you work through the programme and share it with the group. Connect with other people who are undertaking this journey. Offer support and be open to receiving it.

Leaving a legacy for others involves serving yourself as well as others. Do the things you're passionate about, because life is short, and you've got to enjoy it, but never lose your purpose. Surround yourself with people who share your goals and values and who inspire you. Go beyond that and *be* the person who inspires you and others.

My mentor, Jock, inspired and motivated me and helped shape the values that ultimately changed my life. I continue to seek out new mentors in my colleagues and my clients because we all have value and can all learn from one another. My sincere hope is that others see me as a mentor and that I can help change their lives and the lives of those around them. This, I hope, will be my legacy.

CONCLUSION

TIME TO TAKE ACTION

Twelve years from now, your future self is going to thank you for something you did today, for an asset you began to build, a habit you formed, a seed you planted.

Even if you're not sure of where it will lead, today's the day to begin.

—SETH GODIN

You have been empowered with the best tools and frameworks to take full responsibility in your business, body, relationships, and mindset. You are equipped to identify and achieve your vision, execute your 90-Day Reset, and create your own lasting legacy.

You have one shot at this life to live it to your full potential.

It's your responsibility to be the best version of you and inspire others to become their best version of themselves.

No one is going to give you the power to grow your business, get fit and lean, improve your relationships, and develop your mental toughness so you lead the life you should be living. That's 100 per cent down to you!

I know that managing *The 4 Keys* is challenging, and it may seem like you can't keep up at times. Hundreds of business leaders and I are living proof that you can. If we can do it, then so can you!

Now it's your turn. Be one of the few, the brave, forward-thinking leaders who will make real change happen.

—Andrew Sillitoe

AFTERWORD

I'm often asked to provide 1:1 executive coaching and consulting, and I do this through my online training programmes so I can maximise my time and impact more business leaders globally.

I still work with a small number of clients face-to-face and on my annual Get Fit To Win Retreat.

Please say hi over on Instagram and Twitter @andrewsillitoe, as I love to hear what your current business challenges are. Remember, the Get Fit To Win community is always willing to help.

Looking for more assistance with *The 4 Keys* but with video too? Find out more at: AndrewSillitoe.com, such as:

- Thirty-four video lessons covering three areas: *Start*

with a Vision, Turn Your Vision into Reality, and *Live Your Vision.*

- Get clear about your vision and purpose across *The 4 Keys* to lead the life you want.
- Make a new start with the 90-Day Reset and accelerate making your vision a reality.
- Additional hints and tips on effective goal setting to achieve sustainable change.
- Implement a unique system that brings balance back to your life.
- A clear step-by-step online programme that works on all devices.

JOIN THE MASTERMIND?

- Join a network of likeminded entrepreneurs, business owners, and leaders.
- Find out how to maintain thriving personal relationships whilst building a business.
- Get the latest research on sales and marketing tips to grow your business.
- Access the latest research on how to stay lean and get strong and healthy fast.
- Mindset tools to keep your head in the game and thrive every day.
- Monthly video call with Andrew Sillitoe: join the video where Andrew will share latest tips from experts on

how to win in your business, body, relationships, and mindset.

AndrewSillitoe.com

ACKNOWLEDGMENTS

There are plenty of people who helped launch Get Fit To Win and bring *The 4 Keys* book to fruition, and I am grateful to all of them. Once *The 4 Keys* started to go from just a simple idea to changing lives, there were many people involved who deserve to be acknowledged and thanked.

Although I truly believed in the concept, I wasn't entirely sure whether Get Fit To Win was a serious proposition. Ten minutes with Nick Harrington, and I went from an idea to full throttle, and Get Fit To Win was born. Thanks to Nick's incredible energy and encouragement, I went from a concept to something very real within 24 hours!

I want to give a massive shout-out to the Get Fit To Win Mastermind. This is a group of dedicated business leaders who I had the pleasure of experiencing *The 4 Keys* programme with, holding each other accountable and achieving results way beyond our imagination. Their ideas, feedback, and suggestions helped me shape *The 4 Keys* programme into what it is today. You know who you are.

Big thank-you to Rik and Matt at Anorak for their input into the Get Fit To Win brand. They are absolute geniuses and have made it so much fun along the way. Their humour and expertise have made the whole process so enjoyable.

Thanks to everyone on the Scribe team who helped me so much in getting the book outlined, well structured, and published on time. They challenged me throughout to create the best book possible. Thank you, James, Rachel, and Susan!

I have had a very blessed childhood growing up, which I owe a lot to my older siblings, Jacquie, Joanne, Nick, and Spencer. You have all positively influenced my life much more than you realise.

To my godfather, Jock Munn, my first mentor, who helped me understand early in life how the mind can achieve much more when the body wants to give up. During the training sessions on cold winter nights in the damp garage with rusty old weights, he trained me both physically and mentally, and was the inspiration for me to pursue a career in coaching.

Now to the four special people in my life who bring so much joy every day. Izzie, my daughter, who has grown into such a strong, thoughtful, and wise person, and a pretty good skier too! Harry and Freya, who light up my day and bring out the inner child in me. Lucie, an incredible mum to our children, who had the courage to stand up and speak the truth, and without whom this book would never have been written. I love you all.

I have to finish by thanking my caring and awesome mum. From buying me my first hockey stick to allowing me the freedom to be a free thinker and giving me the space to grow as a person, and for always being there to listen and never judge me. Her inner strength and selflessness are inspiring and a legacy that will live forever. Now it's your turn to write your book. Thank you so much. Love you, Mum!

ABOUT THE AUTHOR

ANDREW SILLITOE is a business psychologist, performance coach, public speaker, and author from Kent, England, who doesn't challenge conventional leadership theory. He takes it a step further with an approach that not only changes how we think about leadership but also how we live our lives.

Blending 20 years' experience as an elite international sportsman and coach along with three published books and an acclaimed TEDx Talk, Andrew's innovative and straight-talking views on leadership, teamwork, and strategy have resulted in his advice and guidance being sought after by key figures at FTSE 100 companies. Andrew has worked with more than 3,000 leaders, athletes, and coaches during the last 20 years, and his innovative approach has earned him invitations to work with a range of global companies that include Pfizer, Nationwide, Virgin, and the BBC.

In 1997 Andrew made the move to Canada to pursue a professional roller hockey career and develop his coaching skills. He succeeded in both, becoming the first British player to play professionally while his thriving coaching business was born.

In 2004 he moved into the corporate world as a sales and marketing consultant for Yellow Pages. In 2007 his unique and visionary approach in business saw him headhunted by a consultancy to speak about a 'winning mindset'. It proved the spark that lit his future career path.

Andrew played inline hockey in 11 world championships for Team Great Britain and went on to become the team's head coach. During his four years leading the team, he made history, winning championships in 2011 and 2013, getting into the top eight countries in 2012 and 2014.

Just a year later, he'd developed a new method to enable elite athletes and business leaders to fulfil their potential. This was the seed that eventually blossomed into his renowned *The 4 Keys* approach.

Today, Andrew runs the UK's number one training company for entrepreneurs and business owners who want to fast-track wins in *The 4 Keys*: business, body, relationships, and mindset.

Made in the USA
Las Vegas, NV
04 January 2022

40143246R00150